HORATIO NELSON

and his Valiant Victory

**Written and illustrated by
Philip Reeve**

A division of Scholastic Ltd
London ~ New York ~ Toronto ~ Sydney ~ Auckland
Mexico City ~ New Delhi ~ Hong Kong

First published in the UK by Scholastic Ltd, 2003
This edition published 2011

Text and illustration © Philip Reeve, 2003

ISBN 978 1407 12407 0

Page layout services provided by Quadrum Solutions Ltd, Mumbai, India
Printed and bound in the UK by CPI Bookmarque, Croydon, Surrey

2 4 6 8 10 9 7 5 3

Papers used by Scholastic Children's Books are made from woods grown
in sustainable forests.

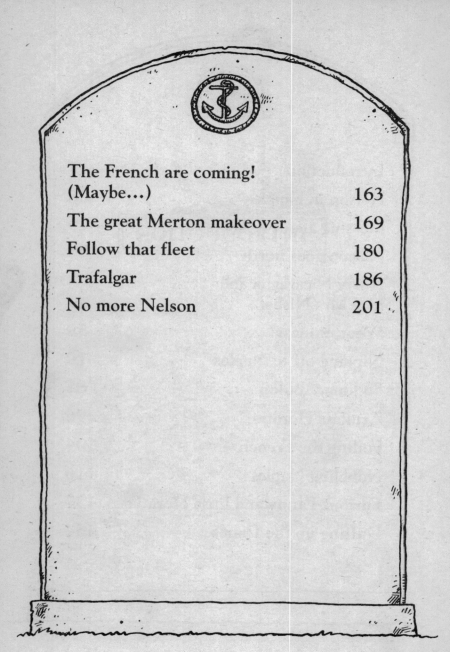

INTRODUCTION

Horatio Nelson was horribly famous when he was alive, and he became even more horribly famous once he was dead. Even now, nearly 200 years later, most people know something about him. We asked a selection of ordinary passers-by what the name Nelson means to them...

MRS RITA HINGE, HOUSEWIFE:
OOH, WASN'T HE A FAMOUS ADMIRAL?

COLUMBA VULGARIS, PIGEON:
HIS HAT MAKES A FANTASTIC LOO!

TRACY CRISP, SCHOOLGIRL:
HE ONLY HAD ONE ARM! AND ONE EYE!

E. B. SPILLAGE, HISTORY TEACHER:
ER...
UM...
NELSON... NELSON... ISN'T THAT THE PUB ON THE HIGH STREET?

N. BONAPARTE, EMPEROR OF FRANCE.

NELSON? PAH! 'E IS NUZZING BUT UN BIG SHOW OFF WITH UN VISAGE LIKE UNE SQUASHED TOMATE. 'OO WANTS TO READ ABURT 'IM? PUT ZIS BOOK DOWN AT WERNSE AND TRY READING ABURT SOMEONE REALLY FAMURSE — LIKE MOI!

Well, if you carry on reading this book, you'll soon know more about Nelson than all that lot put together. It will tell you…

• How he helped to foil Napoleon's invasion of England.
• What his statue is doing on top of a 145-feet-high column in the middle of London.
• Where he lost his arm…
• *And* his eye.

You'll also be able to:

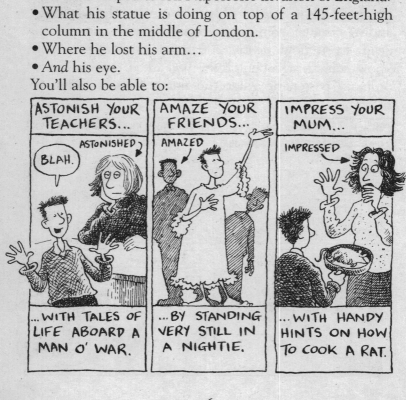

ASTONISH YOUR TEACHERS…

BLAH.

ASTONISHED

…WITH TALES OF LIFE ABOARD A MAN O' WAR.

AMAZE YOUR FRIENDS…

AMAZED

…BY STANDING VERY STILL IN A NIGHTIE.

IMPRESS YOUR MUM…

IMPRESSED

…WITH HANDY HINTS ON HOW TO COOK A RAT.

You'll be able to read about Nelson's amazing exploits in the pages of the sensational daily, *The Solar Orb*, and leaf through his secret lost log books, which were recently discovered bobbing about in a bottle just off Blackpool pier, and are *not* just made up, HONEST. You'll even learn the truth about those famous last words...

But we don't get to that until a bit later on...

First come 193 action-packed pages of exciting battles, passionate *lurve* and very nasty dinners...

NELSON IN NAPPIES

On 29th September 1758, at the little village of Burnham Thorpe in Norfolk, something happened that sounded a bit like this:

Of course, if the midwife had read this book, she'd have been able to say:

...but she hadn't. In fact, nobody could have guessed that little Horatio would go on to become a famous hero. In those days most famous heroes came from rich and powerful families and the Nelsons weren't rich or powerful.

Horatio's father, Edmund Nelson, was the rector of Burnham Thorpe. He was a quiet, shy man who never travelled far from the village except for the few years he spent at Cambridge University studying to be a clergyman. In 1749 he had married Horatio's mother, Catherine Suckling. She was related to a powerful Norfolk family called the Walpoles.

I MAY HAVE A SILLY-SOUNDING SURNAME, BUT MY GRANDMOTHER'S BROTHER WAS SIR ROBERT WALPOLE, WHO WAS THE FIRST PRIME MINISTER OF ENGLAND!

The Walpoles owned a lot of land around Burnham Thorpe, and it was thanks to them that Edmund had got his job as rector. The Nelsons sucked up to their rich relations, and that was how the new baby came to be called Horatio...

BURP!

WE'LL NAME HIM AFTER LORD WALPOLE'S FATHER!

...although when he got a bit older, Horatio decided that he didn't much like his name...

> HORATIO'S A STUPID NAME! I WANT A COOL-SOUNDING NAME, LIKE... ER... I KNOW! **HORACE!**

...and he got his way. As well as Horatio – sorry, Horace – the Nelsons had seven other children; four boys and three girls. We'd better introduce the family, so you can see what he had to deal with.

But Horace's most interesting relative was his mother's brother, Captain Maurice Suckling of the Royal Navy. He was the one that Suckling Nelson was named after...

> OH, THANKS A BUNCH, UNCLE MAURICE!

...and he was also a bit of a hero. In the year Horace was born, Britain had been fighting the Seven Years War against France, and Uncle Maurice had led a squadron of British warships which defeated a much larger French squadron in the Caribbean. In those days officers who won sea battles were rewarded with part of the value of any ships they captured, and Uncle Maurice had done quite nicely out of his victory and bought himself a country house. He was a regular visitor to Burnham Thorpe and Horace and his brothers and sisters grew up with his tales of life at sea.

GO ON, UNCLE MAURICE, TELL US HOW YOU BEAT THE FRENCH...

OH, IT WAS NOTHING...

OH, PLEASE, PLEASE, PLEASE, PLEASE, PLEASE, PLEASE, PLEASE, PLEASE, PLEASE, PLEASE, PLEASE, PLEASE, PLEASE!

WELL, ACTUALLY I ONCE CAPTURED 27 SHIPS SINGLE-HANDED...

It was probably listening to his uncle that first made young Horace dream of becoming a sailor himself. It didn't seem very likely that it would ever happen, though, because he was turning out to be a rather sickly, delicate boy, and quite small for his age. But he was very brave, and could easily see off his bullying older brothers. Once, his sister Susannah was asked to stop Horace and William fighting because William was so much bigger and stronger. She just said:

OH, LET THEM ALONE. LITTLE HORATIO WILL FLATTEN HIM.

IT'S HORACE ACTUALLY!

Then, on Boxing Day 1767, something terrible happened.

CHILDREN, YOUR MOTHER IS DEAD.

OH NO!

MUMMY!

NOW WHO'LL HELP US EAT ALL THESE LEFT-OVER TURKEY SANDWICHES?

Horace was only nine years old, and he never really got over losing his mother. And poor Edmund Nelson was left to bring up eight children on his own!

The rector was a kindly man, but he believed children needed firm discipline. (He made Horace and the others sit up straight by forbidding them from letting their spines touch the backs of their chairs.) The school he chose for the boys (Paston School, in nearby North Walsham) was famous for its tough headmaster, a stern Welsh clergyman called John Price Jones. There Horace learned Latin and Greek, and probably got caned a lot as well, since Mr Jones was a firm believer in flogging.

Most of the stories about Horace's childhood make him out to be SUPERBOY. His granny told one about the time he got lost in the countryside near Burnham Thorpe. He finally found his way home and she said…

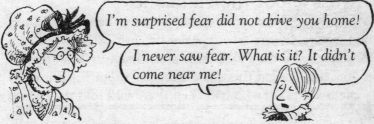

I'm surprised fear did not drive you home!

I never saw fear. What is it? It didn't come near me!

But if you ask me, Granny made that one up.

Then there was the time Horace and his brother William set off for school through a blizzard. Edmund Nelson told them not to turn back unless they were sure there was no way of reaching the school. After a little way William wanted to give up, but Horace wouldn't hear of it.

Remember, brother, it was left to our honour.

If he'd been my brother he'd have got a snowball up the hooter. But there is one story of Horace getting into (gasp) trouble at school. The boys in his dormitory wanted to pinch some nice juicy pears from Mr Jones's orchard; the only problem was, they were too scared of the dreaded Welsh whacker to sneak in there. Horace volunteered, and was lowered out of the window on a rope made of knotted sheets to do the dirty deed. He succesfully got back with the pilfered pears, but he was far too much of a goody-goody to actually eat any; he'd only gone on the pear-pinching expedition to prove that he was a bit of a hero.

A fuss about the Falklands

Meanwhile, there was trouble brewing between Britain and Spain. In the South Atlantic, just off the coast of Argentina, lie the Falkland Islands. Back in 1764 British sailors had landed there and declared them British, even though a captain who had been there said that they were:

Nothing but bog and barren mountains, beaten by storms almost perpetual.

But in 1770 the Spanish (who already controlled much of South America) landed on the islands themselves and pulled down the British flag. The Brits were furious. They were sure that they were Top Nation, and they weren't going to let a bunch of foreigners get away with this sort of thing...

THE SOLAR ORB
NO WAY, JOSÉ

1770

Do those sneaky Spaniards think they can nick our islands and get away with it? The Falklands may only be a few bleak bogs and mountains where nobody lives, but they're OUR bleak bogs and mountains where nobody lives!

They're also home to huge colonies of PENGUINS, and we all know how the slimy Spaniards treat penguins…

Britons! Are you prepared to let flightless British sea birds fall into the hands of Spain? The Seven Years War proved that we've got the BEST NAVY IN THE WHOLE WORLD! Isn't it time our brave boys in blue[1] showed the savage senors a thing or two?

The Orb says: THIS MEANS WAR!

1. All right, blue and white. And a sort of sludgy brown colour.

BODGETT & CO.
Suppliers of Enormous Hats.

GET AHEAD – GET A HAT.

The Royal Navy started to prepare for a fight. Ships were made ready, and 12-year-old Horatio – whoops, Horace – heard that his Uncle Maurice had been put in command of a 64-gun warship called the *Raisonable*, which was being prepared to go and help recapture the Falkland Islands. He knew this was the chance he had been waiting for. He persuaded his father to write to Uncle Maurice and ask if there was room for a small Nelson on the voyage.

Maurice Suckling wrote back:

What has poor Horatio done, who is so weak, that he should be sent to rough it out at sea? But let him come. The first time we go into action a cannon ball may knock his head off and provide for him at once!

And so, on the 1st January 1771, young Horace's name was entered on the *Raisonnable's* muster-book as a midshipman – the first step on the way to becoming a captain.

STOP CALLING ME HORACE! NOW I'M IN THE NAVY I WANT A GLORIOUS, HEROIC SOUNDING NAME, LIKE, ER... **HORATIO!**

Oh, suit yourself. Technically, Horace – I mean, Horatio – wasn't even qualified to be a midshipman, as this was his first voyage. But since the *Raisonnable's* captain was his uncle, nobody was about to argue.

It's hard to imagine why anybody would have wanted to sail aboard a warship in 1771. The food was foul, the floggings were frequent and if you didn't drown or die of disease you had a good chance of being blown to bits in a battle. For ordinary people, though, that was sometimes an improvement on life ashore. This was a time when labourers in the countryside were paid such low wages that many were almost starving, and others were being booted off their land by changes in farming. In the cities, conditions in the new mills and factories were as bad as anything at sea; if the machinery didn't mangle you, the disease and pollution would probably finish you off. And if you chucked a brick through the boss's window by way of complaint he could have you whipped or put in the stocks or packed off to a prison colony on the far side of the world.

Of course, Horatio didn't have to escape from anything like this – his family might not be rich, but nobody was going to make him slave over a steam-powered triple-action rotary orphan-squasher at

Grimethwaite's Grommeting Mill. No, if he'd stayed on land he might have ended up as something far, far worse ... a COUNTRY VICAR!

As Horatio boarded the stagecoach that would take him to join his uncle's ship at Chatham docks, he knew that the Royal Navy was his best chance of getting away from boring old Burnham Thorpe, winning wealth and finding fame.

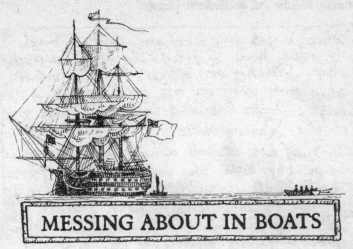

MESSING ABOUT IN BOATS

Horatio travelled with his father as far as London, then said his goodbyes and went on alone to the docks at Chatham, where the ship was getting ready to sail.

The Secret Log Book of H. Nelson.

10th March 1771

Tossing, jolting, rolling, pitching up and down, side to side... feeling a bit sick already... and I'm not even at sea yet – this is just the coach that's taking me to Chatham! It's a six-hour journey, and once you leave London the roads are very rough ... 'scuse me...

Sick →

Later.

Well, this isn't the welcome I'd expected. There was nobody waiting to meet me when I got to Chatham and I had no idea how to find Uncle Maurice's ship. Finally an officer from another ship took pity on me and found a boat to take me and my sea-chest out to the Raisonnable.

She's not at all what I imagined. From the boat she looked like a great dark wall of sodden wood towering up out of the water, with square lids over the gun ports and a little narrow ladder going up the side. It was difficult to climb, and I was afraid I'd fall into the gap between the boat and the ship and drown, but I didn't want the common sailors to think I was a coward, so I ran up as quick as I could.

ME

Once I got on deck I found that nobody aboard knew I was coming! Uncle Maurice is away, and won't be back for a few days. The officer in charge showed me to the midshipmen's berth, which I'll be sharing with about 24 other boys during the voyage. It's down under the water-line – a dark little low-beamed hole that stinks of mould and tar.

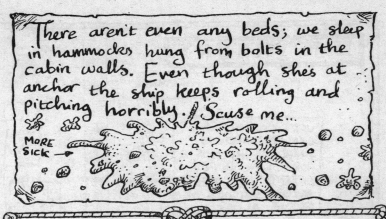

There aren't even any beds; we sleep in hammocks hung from bolts in the cabin walls. Even though she's at anchor the ship keeps rolling and pitching horribly. Scuse me...

MORE SICK →

ALL AT SEA ⌁ SHIP SHAPE

Life on a Royal Navy ship in the 18th century must have come as a shock to young Horatio. It was like wandering into a different world. As another midshipman recalled, 'All seemed strange, different language and strange expressions of tongue, that I thought myself always asleep or in a dream, and never properly awake.'

The Navy used all sorts of small vessels like brigs, sloops and schooners, but the most important ships were:

- Ships-of-the-line: large two- or three-decker warships which carried 64–100 cannons. They were used for fighting full-scale battles.
- Frigates: smaller, faster ships with 20–50 guns.

Before we go any further, let's take a look at the most famous ship-of-the-line Nelson ever served on (although she didn't become his flagship until 1803), the 100-gun HMS VICTORY.

HMS VICTORY

FOREMAST.

VERTICAL ROPES CALLED 'SHROUDS' SUPPORT THE MASTS. HORIZONTAL ROPES CALLED 'RATLINES' ALLOW SAILORS TO CLIMB ALOFT.

SHIP'S BOATS.

SHIP'S BELL.

'ROUNDHOUSE'- TOILET FOR JUNIOR OFFICERS.

'SEATS OF EASE'- OPEN AIR LOOS FOR THE SAILORS.

LOWER GUN DECK

PLATFORMS HALFWAY UP EACH MAST, CALLED 'TOPS' WERE USED BY SAILORS WORKING ON THE RIGGING, AND BY MARINE SHARP-SHOOTERS IN BATTLE.

OFFICERS COMMANDED THE SHIP FROM THE QUARTERDECK.

CAPTAINS AND ADMIRALS HAD POSH CABINS AT THE STERN OF THE SHIP.

VERY COSY!

THE COMMON SAILORS SLEPT AND ATE ON THE MIDDLE AND LOWER GUN DECKS.

KEEP THE BLOOMIN' NOISE DOWN!

THE 'COCKPIT', WHICH WAS ON THE ORLOP DECK, JUST ABOVE THE HOLD, WAS THE SHIP'S SURGERY IN TIMES OF BATTLE.

OW!

THE HOLD – BELOW THE WATERLINE AT THE VERY BOTTOM OF THE SHIP – WAS A STORAGE SPACE FOR FOOD, WATER, SPARE PARTS, GUNPOWDER...

AND RATS!

A ship of this size needed a big crew just to shift all those sails – and an even bigger one to fight with in battle. The crew was arranged in a very strict order. Top of the heap was:

The **captain** (or post captain, as he was called in Horatio's day – the 'post' bit was later dropped). The captain was completely responsible for the ship and everyone aboard. He had to know enough about the wind and weather and the way the ship worked to get where he wanted to go, and enough about fighting to defeat the enemy when he got there. On the plus side, he got the best cabin all to himself – but he was expected to entertain other officers and visitors at his own expense, which was all very well if he was as rich as Maurice Suckling, but not so good if he only had his pay to live on.

The **first lieutenant** was next down: the second in command, who was expected to take over the running of the ship if the captain was absent, ill, injured or killed. Up to six other **lieutenants** helped with the running of the ship and commanded sections of guns in battle. They were usually young officers, waiting for the chance to become captains with a ship of their own. But to be promoted you either needed to have friends in high places or to have done something brave enough to get mentioned in your captain's report after a battle – and there were plenty of unlucky old lieutenants who never did make it to the top.

Midshipmen: this was Horatio's rank – a sort of trainee sea officer, often as young as eight or nine. If you survived being a mid you could take an exam to qualify for promotion to lieutenant.

Warrant officers: these were skilled seamen with particular jobs to do aboard the ship. The **gunner** was in charge of the guns, shot and powder, the **purser** was in charge of pay and supplies, the **boatswain** (or bosun) looked after sails and rigging, the **master** helped the captain navigate and the **surgeon** did his best to look after the crew. If you were lucky your ship's surgeon might be a trained doctor. If not, you might end up with a vet, or even a former butcher. Either way, there often wasn't much more he could do than saw off injured arms and legs and bandage bloody wounds.

Inferior warrant officers and **petty officers** included the cook, the sail maker, the armourer (in charge of weapons and acting as a sort of floating blacksmith, responsible for all the ship's metalwork) plus assistants to the other officers and warrant officers.

Marines were not sailors but soldiers, armed with swords and muskets. In battle they were used to shoot at the crew of enemy ships – especially the officers on the quarterdeck. The rest of the time they helped the officers keep control of...

The **seamen** or 'ratings': the bottom of the heap. There were about 850 aboard the *Victory*, divided into two 'watches' or shifts (one watch worked the ship while the other watch was asleep). Some were experienced sailors, called **able seamen**. The rest were **ordinary seamen**, with little or no experience of shipboard life. Unlike the officers, who were all Brits, the common seamen came from as far afield as Poland, India, Africa, America; even from Britain's old enemies, France and Spain. Manpower was sometimes so short that the numbers

would be made up with men brought in from prisons and madhouses. (And some might not be men at all; there were several cases of women joining the navy in disguise. At least two women, Mary Ann Riley and Jane Hopping, fought with Nelson at the Battle of the Nile. Later, in the reign of Queen Victoria, they applied to be given medals like the other veterans, but unfortunately she turned them down.)

In a ship this big, with so many people aboard, it was very important that everyone did as they were told and obeyed their officers without even thinking about it. The middle of a storm or battle was no place for a discussion. That's why the Royal Navy had evolved some pretty strict ways of punishing people. (WARNING: Don't let your teachers see this next bit – it might give them ideas.)

CRIME	PUNISHMENT
Mutiny	Death
Desertion (running away)	Death
Drunkenness	Flogging
Answering back to a senior officer	Flogging
Theft	Flogging
Falling asleep on duty	Flogging
Uncleanliness (going to the loo where you weren't supposed to...)	Flogging

Flogging meant strapping the offender to a grating and whacking him across the bare back with a thin, nine-stranded whip called the cat-o'-nine-tails. Of course, some captains were stricter than others. Some didn't like flogging, and tried to find other punishments for small offences – like chaining the offender up in 'irons' or making him 'Lord of the Heads' (in charge of cleaning out the toilets). Others thought a good bit of flogging kept the crew on its toes and would sometimes sentence men to as many as 50 lashes – more than enough to kill most people.

One of the midshipmen's jobs was enforcing this sort of discipline, as Horatio would have discovered as he settled down to life aboard the *Raisonnable*...

The Secret Log Book of H. Nelson
27th March 1771

Still moored in the Medway. I'm getting used to life aboard ship, and the rolling and tossing doesn't make me feel so sick now. Uncle Maurice is back on board, and we've been preparing for the voyage, loading the store rooms with salt beef, butter, cheese, biscuit and beer. Also we've been bringing the guns aboard; ferrying them out on a barge and winching them onto the ship using a block and tackle. It seems strange to be ordering great big sailors about — some of them are older than Father, and have been all round the world, and I'm telling them what to do even though I'm only 12 and have never been to sea. But Uncle Maurice says I'm a gentleman and they're just common sailors, so it's all right.

Yesterday we had to punish some men for drunkenness and disobedience. The whole crew watched while the bosun's mate tied them to a grating and gave them each nine strokes of the cat. The whip tore the skin off their backs, and there was a lot of blood to be mopped off the deck afterwards. Still, Uncle Maurice says that it's the only way to keep discipline aboard ship.

All the guns and stores are finally aboard. Soon we'll get our orders to sail for the South Atlantic and WAR! (Hurrah!)

10th April 1771

Terrible news! The war's off! Government has settled the Falkland Islands row peacefully, and the poor old Raisonnable is going to stay anchored here at Chatham until the Admiralty decide what's to be done with her. The sailors are all celebrating, but I don't see anything to be happy about. I was looking forward to fighting the Spanish. I was going to make a name for myself and bring back lots of prize money.

Now what am I going to do?

Horatio learns the ropes

Uncle Maurice was put in command of a guard ship called the *Triumph*, which was anchored off the mouth of the Thames – more like a floating fortress than a warship. But he thought Horatio needed some time at sea to turn him into a real sailor. Luckily, one of his old shipmates commanded a merchant ship which traded with Britain's colonies in the Caribbean, and he was happy to take Horatio on as a junior officer.

Life aboard a merchantman was very different from what Horatio had seen aboard the *Raisonnable*. There was no punishment, and the gap between officers and men was not so great. The sailors were kind to him, and as he got to know them he came to realize that they hated the Royal Navy. In times of war the Navy was often short of experienced sailors, who didn't want to endure the danger and discipline of life on a warship when they could earn more on a merchantman. So the Navy sent teams of men called 'press gangs' to scour British harbours and homecoming ships. If they found a seaman who wasn't already in the Navy they were allowed to 'impress' him...

Sometimes the press gangs beat people unconscious or got them drunk before they dragged them aboard ship – and the poor victim didn't wake up until he was far from land. Sometimes a merchant ship would be stopped on the way back from a long voyage and have part of its crew nabbed for the Navy. Men pressed into service in this way were often at sea for four or five years at a stretch, leaving behind families and friends who might have no idea what had become of them!

Later, Horatio said of this first voyage:

I returned ... with a horror of the Royal Navy. It was many weeks before I got in the least reconciled to a man o' war.

Horatio spent nearly a year aboard the merchant ship, and came back a much better sailor. Uncle Maurice put him in charge of a longboat which ran errands between the *Triumph* and the shore, sometimes taking messages right up the Thames to London. It was on one of these trips that Horatio noticed two ships being prepared for sea at the dockyards of Sheerness and Deptford. He asked around at the docks, and found out that they were the *Carcass* and the *Racehorse*, and that they were being made ready for an important expedition.

AHARR, HORATIO LAD! THEY BE BOUND FOR THE ARCTIC!

BRRRR!

THE ARCTIC! THAT SOUNDS MORE EXCITING THAN FERRYING MESSAGES UP AND DOWN THE THAMES! I'M GOING TO APPLY TO SAIL WITH THEM!

WRAP UP NICE AND WARM, THEN.

NELSON GOES NORTH

The Secret Log Book of H. Nelson

4th June 1773

We're off! At first light today we made sail and steered north, while England vanished into the fog behind us. We're off to search for a way of getting to Japan and China by sailing through the icy seas north of Russia. Nobody is sure if it's possible, but if it is it will mean that ships can sail into the Pacific without having to go all the way round the bottom of South America and risk foundering in the horrible tempests and hurricanes off Cape Horn.

The expedition is led by Captain the Honourable Constantine Phipps, who is commanding the Racehorse. (My ship, the Carcass, is commanded by Captain Lutwidge.) As well as searching for the north-east passage we are testing out a lot of new scientific equipment, like a "PATENT MACHINE FOR MAKING SEA WATER DRINKABLE" and a "NEW DEVICE FOR MEASURING A SHIP'S SPEED". And the great naturalist Sir Joseph Banks, who is a friend of Captain Phipps, has asked us to make notes on the arctic wildlife: fish, seals, whales and terrible white bears!

10th July

Yesterday we saw our first ice-mountains. They are huge, drifting islands of ice; very pretty to look at, but they could easily sink our little ships if we do not keep clear. Today there is a lot of pack ice floating on the surface of the sea, and away to the north we can see great smooth plains of ice stretching for miles and miles.

On one of the ice floes we saw walruses – strange creatures like something out of a seafarer's yarn; as fat and blubbery as my brother Maurice and nearly as ugly.

MAURICE →   WALRUS →   Yuk!

Some of our scientific gentlemen took one of the boats and went for a closer look. When they fired at one of the brutes with their muskets, its friends came sliding down off the ice and attacked them, crashing against the sides of their boat with such violence that they would have surely sunk. Luckily I had the presence of mind to launch a second boat and drive them away. Hurrah for me!

OUR HERO!   SHOO   GRRR   SNARL

Bear-faced cheek

Walruses were only the start of Horatio's arctic adventures. A few weeks later (according to one story) Horatio and another midshipman decided to go ashore and hunt a polar bear. They hadn't got permission to leave the ship, but they managed to sneak away in a small boat, armed only with a rusty musket...

Captain Lutwidge was furious with Horatio for disobeying orders and nearly getting himself eaten, but he couldn't help but be impressed by the boy's bravery. In later years he would often tell the story of Nelson and the bear.

By the end of July, Horatio had more than bears to worry about. The arctic summer was ending, and soon both ships were trapped by the spreading ice. Far from land, supplies of fresh food were running low – and Navy food wasn't exactly *cordon bleu* at the best of times (more like *cordon bleeeugh!*).

ALL AT SEA: DISMAL DINNERS

What you ate on board ship depended on where it was. The Royal Navy had discovered that sailors needed a good supply of vitamin C from fresh fruit and veg. Without it, they might go down with **scurvy**: they would grow increasingly weak, their muscles would ache, their teeth would drop out, years-old wounds would re-open and eventually they'd die. For this reason, navy ships always tried to lay in stocks of fresh food when they came near land. Also, most set off with a small menagerie of farm animals aboard; cows, pigs, sheep and chickens were not unusual sights on an 18th-century man o' war. But voyages could last months or even years and, once the fresh stuff was used up and the animals had been scoffed, crew and officers alike had to fall back on basic rations.

The typical food rations for one sailor for a week were:

MENU

12 oz CHEESE  (Probably hard and very smelly.)

7lb BISCUIT (No nice Jammy Dodgers – ship's biscuit was a sort of hard, dry bread.)

2lb PORK AND **4lb BEEF**  (Meat was salted to preserve it. It might have been kicking around the hold for years before it landed on your plate.)

3pts SKILLYGALEE (OATMEAL PORRIDGE)

 Mmm! Lovely!

PLUS **BUTTER, DRIED PEAS** AND SOMETIMES **PICKLED CABBAGE** TO KEEP THE SCURVY AT BAY.

There were a few things that an enterprising young midshipman could do to liven up the basic menu. Ship's biscuit was home to fat, black-headed maggots called 'bargemen', which turned into weevils when they grew up.

BARGEMAN WEEVIL

HEH HEH HEH! SOON THE WHOLE BISCUIT WILL BE MINE!

EVIL WEEVIL

Some people thumped their biscuit on the table before eating to dislodge the little visitors, but most didn't bother. Bargemen were juicy, and weevils were crunchy and bitter.

If that's set your mouth watering, how about a nice rat for seconds? All 18th-century ships were home to whole families of rats (sometimes called 'Millers' because they had a knack of getting into the storerooms and scoffing all the flour). If you could catch a few, they'd make a nice change from all that salt beef and pork, and could be cooked in the midshipmen's mess. And if you were nice to the cook he might give you some 'slush' to fry them in. (Slush was the yellowish grease that bobbed to the surface of the cauldron while he was cooking the meat. It also came in handy for spreading on ship's biscuit when the butter ran out.)

Right, that's dinner sorted, but what's to drink? Well, there's a daily ration of lime or lemon juice to stop scurvy, and the nice old Navy also allows each man seven gallons of beer a week. That might seem like a lot – it's a wonder anybody could see straight to sail the ship – but it's better than drinking the water (which is stale and full of slimy green algae and other nasties). Then there's a drink of rum as a reward when the crew has worked particularly hard, and when the crew went ashore on leave most of them spent their hard-earned pay on … more drink!

Occasionally a crew would get so drunk that a ship was completely disabled. But at sea, where a single slip-up could mean disaster for the whole ship, drunkenness was a crime and most men seem to have downed their gallon a day without getting too tipsy.

Ups and downs

Horatio and the others aboard *Racehorse* and *Carcass* had more to moan about than nauseating nosh. The ice-sheets were closing in all around them, and for a while it looked as if the ships would be crushed and this book would only be 41 pages long. Then, luckily, an east wind blew up, parting the ice just enough for them to escape. They headed home, and by the end of September they were safe in Deptford Reach.

The expedition had been a bit of a failure really. It hadn't reached any further north than other ships had been, and it certainly hadn't reached Japan and China.

But it had given Horatio his first real taste of adventure – and when he got home, Uncle Maurice kindly arranged a second helping.

This time he was to sail aboard a frigate called the *Seahorse*, on a voyage that couldn't have been more different from the trip to the Arctic. She was to sail east and join the squadron of ships which protected British shipping in the seas around India.

The voyage lasted two years. By the time Horatio came home again he had:

• Taken part in his first battle (against a ship belonging to Hyder Ali, an Indian prince who was an ally of the French).

• Won £300 in a game of cards (a HUGE amount of money in those days – and when Horatio thought about what would have happened if he had lost, it made him give up gambling for good).

• Caught malaria.

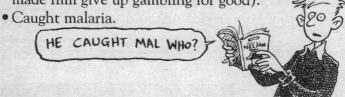

HE CAUGHT MAL WHO?

Malaria. It's a very serious tropical disease, spread by the bite of the anopheles mosquito – but at the end of the 18th century nobody knew that, and most doctors thought that it was caused by bad air rising off swamps. And not only did they not know what caused it – they hadn't had much luck treating it either. The surgeon of the *Seahorse* decided that Horatio's best chance of survival was to return to England. He was transferred aboard another frigate, the *Dolphin*, for a gentle voyage home. He was probably expecting something like this…

Unfortunately it turned out to be more like this...

For Horatio, down in the sickbay, it must have been a nightmare.

He very nearly died, but luckily for us, he didn't. The *Dolphin* sailed into calmer waters at last and stopped off for a month at the Cape of Good Hope. By the time it sailed on again, Horatio was back on his feet and his health was beginning to mend. But he wasn't a happy Horatio…

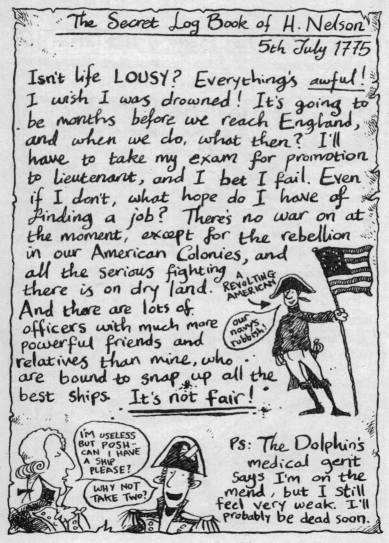

The Secret Log Book of H. Nelson

5th July 1775

Isn't life LOUSY? Everything's awful! I wish I was drowned! It's going to be months before we reach England, and when we do, what then? I'll have to take my exam for promotion to Lieutenant, and I bet I fail. Even if I don't, what hope do I have of finding a job? There's no war on at the moment, except for the rebellion in our American Colonies, and all the serious fighting there is on dry land. And there are lots of officers with much more powerful friends and relatives than mine, who are bound to snap up all the best ships. It's not fair!

A REVOLTING AMERICAN

our navy's rubbish!

I'M USELESS BUT POSH- CAN I HAVE A SHIP PLEASE?

WHY NOT TAKE TWO?

Ps: The Dolphin's medical gent says I'm on the mend, but I still feel very weak. I'll probably be dead soon.

The fact was, Horatio's illness had left him seriously depressed. But as the *Dolphin* sailed onward something strange was about to happen that would change his whole outlook on life.

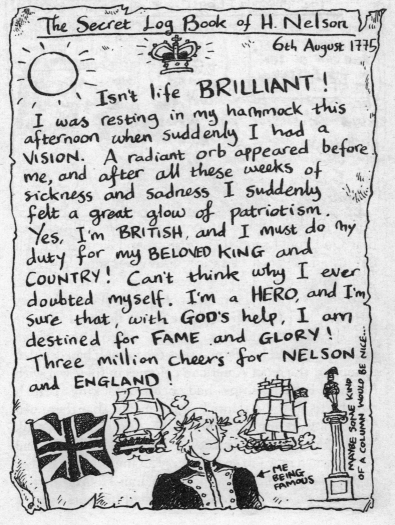

The Secret Log Book of H. Nelson

6th August 1775

Isn't life BRILLIANT!
I was resting in my hammock this afternoon when suddenly I had a VISION. A radiant orb appeared before me, and after all these weeks of sickness and sadness I suddenly felt a great glow of patriotism. Yes, I'm BRITISH, and I must do my duty for my BELOVED KING and COUNTRY! Can't think why I ever doubted myself. I'm a HERO, and I'm sure that, with GOD's help, I am destined for FAME and GLORY! Three million cheers for NELSON and ENGLAND!

← ME BEING FAMOUS

MAYBE SOME KIND OF A COLUMN WOULD BE NICE...

Horatio's vision is one of the oddest parts of his story. You can imagine what would happen today if you went around telling people you'd had visions of radiant orbs.

But in the late 18th century many people still believed that God could send them visions and signs if He felt like it, and even if Horatio's vision was more patriotic than religious it didn't necessarily mean that he was bonkers. Anyway, Horatio took his radiant orb very seriously, and from then on he never doubted that he was special. Happily for Horatio, when the *Dolphin* reached England he learned that the French had decided to support the rebel American colonies in their war with Britain. French ships had been attacking British merchants in the Atlantic, which meant that there was plenty of work for the Royal Navy. And that wasn't all. While Horatio had been away, his Uncle Maurice had been given a new job and was now an important member of the Navy Board – the people whom Horatio had to impress if he was going to be promoted to lieutenant.

Secret Log Book of H Nelson

9th April 1777

My big day! This morning I presented myself at the Admiralty, taking along all my references from my former captains. I had to wait for ages, but at last I was shown into a large, forbidding-looking room where some large, forbidding-looking men sat behind a long table – and one of them was Uncle Maurice! But he just looked at me as if he had never seen me before. Then they all started asking me questions. I was pretty nervous at first, but the questions were really simple!

After a little time they said they had heard enough. Then Uncle Maurice turned to the others and introduced me as his nephew! They were amazed! They didn't understand why Uncle M had not said who I was before, but he explained that he did not want me to be favoured, but 'I felt convinced he would pass a good examination and you see, gentlemen, I have not been disappointed.'

That was when I knew for sure that I had passed! I am now Lieutenant Horatio Nelson of the Royal Navy. Next stop, Fame and Fortune!

NASTY NICARAGUA AND NICE MRS NISBET

The day after his exam, Horatio was given a new job. He was to sail as second lieutenant aboard the frigate *Lowestoffe*, commanded by Captain William Locker. Captain Locker had fought in the Seven Years War, and he was able to teach Horatio a lot about the difficult and dangerous business of fighting at sea.

The *Lowestoffe* was bound for Jamaica, where it was to stop and capture merchant ships from the revolting Americans and help protect British colonies in the West Indies against possible attacks by the French. Soon Horatio was being brave and heroic all over the place, and it wasn't long before he came to the attention of the admiral in command of the Navy's Jamaica Station, who promoted him to command the brig *Badger*. His

BADGER? THAT DOESN'T SOUND VERY HEROIC...

speedy promotion may have been partly due to Uncle Maurice's influence with the Admiralty – but if so, it was the last time Uncle Maurice would be able to help:

Had I been near him, he would have said to me, 'My boy, I leave you to my country; serve her well...'

But with or without an influential uncle, Horatio was going places. In 1779 he was promoted to post captain, and sent off to escort a convoy of troopships to attack a Spanish fort in Nicaragua.

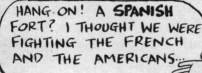

HANG ON! A **SPANISH** FORT? I THOUGHT WE WERE FIGHTING THE FRENCH AND THE AMERICANS...

SCRATCH SCRATCH

Ah, yes, but now the Spanish had declared war on Britain too, and the Brits fancied capturing some of Spain's colonies in South America to replace the ones they were losing in the north. They also had plans to dig a canal right across Nicaragua so that ships could sail through into the Pacific without having to go round the nasty storm-swept pointy bit at the bottom of South America, which could take months and months and was dreadfully tedious.

YOU'RE TELLING US!

Unfortunately, the attack on Nicaragua turned into a DISASTER. Horatio was only supposed to be escorting the British troops to the mouth of the San Juan River. From there, they would make their own way upstream to attack an important Spanish fort, the Castle of San Juan. But when he saw the soldiers' clumsy attempts to load their boats he realized that they would never make it up the dangerous, fast-flowing river without him, and decided he would have to go along and lend a hand. But even with his help, the journey was a nightmare.

THE BOATS KEPT RUNNING AGROUND.

OOPS!

BONK!

STODGE!

BOTHER!

SPLONK!

THE SOLDIERS WERE BITTEN BY MOSQUITOES, LEECHES AND POISONOUS SNAKES.

EUGH! A LEECH!

WHEN THEY FINALLY REACHED THE CASTLE, HORATIO RECOMMENDED A SPEEDY FRONTAL ASSAULT, BUT THE OFFICER IN CHARGE DISAGREED.

OOH, I'M NOT SURE THAT WOULD WORK...

THE MEN SENT TO CAPTURE THE HIGH GROUND BEHIND THE CASTLE WERE UNABLE TO HACK THEIR WAY THROUGH THE DENSE JUNGLE.

I'M REALLY HACKED OFF!

ON THE WAY BACK, ONE OF THE MEN WAS ATTACKED BY A JAGUAR.

EEEEE!

IT MUST BE AN EEEE-TYPE JAGUAR.

HORATIO HELPED SET UP CANNON TO BOMBARD THE CASTLE - BUT THE AMMUNITION RAN OUT.

PANTS!

HA HA!

REINFORCEMENTS WERE SENT FROM THE COAST... BUT LOST MOST OF THEIR SUPPLIES WHEN THEIR BOATS CAPSIZED.

IF YOU CAN READ THIS, YOUR BOAT IS THE WRONG WAY UP.

WHOOPS

MEN STARTED TO FALL ILL WITH DYSENTERY AND MALARIA... AND JUST WHEN EVERYBODY THOUGHT IT COULDN'T GET ANY WORSE, IT STARTED TO RAIN...

SNIFFLE

GROAN!

GRIPE.

Horatio was ill, too, with a fever he'd caught up the San Juan River – but for him, relief was in sight; orders arrived telling him to report back to Jamaica. He was near death by the time he reached Kingston, the island's capital, but luckily one of his friends, Captain Cornwallis of the *Lion*, made sure that he wasn't sent to hospital (where most of the patients came out dead). Instead, he went to stay with Cuba Cornwallis, a former slave whom Captain Cornwallis had freed. She now ran a boarding house, where she dosed Horatio with her herbal remedies and put a nice warm brick in his bed to keep his tootsies toasty when the fever chilled him. (WARNING: Don't try this at home.)

Meanwhile, back in the Nicaraguan jungle, everything was going avocado-shaped. The Castle of San Juan did eventually surrender, but the Brits were so ill and short of food that they had to retreat back to the coast anyway. The attack on Nicaragua had cost the lives of nearly 2,000 soldiers, and 1,000 sailors died aboard the ships which were waiting off the river's mouth to take the survivors home. But even though the whole affair had been a catastrophe, nobody could complain about Horatio's part in it; everyone agreed that he had been brave, intelligent and useful, and some people thought the whole thing might have gone better if the officers in charge had paid more attention to his advice.

Horatio, modest as ever, agreed.

Some chums

Horatio went home to England to recover. As soon as he was well enough he was appointed to command other ships, on voyages to Denmark and Canada, protecting British merchantmen. But the war with the Americans, Spanish and French was winding down, and when Horatio returned to the West Indies in 1784 he wasn't there to fight, just to stop Americans from trading with the British colonists.

The plan was that by refusing to let the Americans trade they would be starved into submission. The problem was that the British colonists wanted to trade with them. American ships often put into West Indian harbours for repairs and provisions. Once they were there, they would ask permission to sell just enough of their cargo to pay for the supplies they needed – and the customs officers would pretend not to notice while they off-loaded stuff.

The other naval officers in the area had pretty much given up trying to stop the trade with America, but Nelson wasn't going to stand for it. He set about turning back any Americans who he found heading for British ports. This made him very unpopular with the local merchants, whose trade he was spoiling, and with some of his fellow officers, who thought he was a bit of a goody-goody.

Luckily, he did have a few friends in the West Indies. Let's have a look at them…

Prince William

William was a son of British King George III; he was also a captain in the Royal Navy, and he had met Horatio on his first stay in the West Indies. He thought young Nelson was fantastic – and Horatio, who had a bit of a soft spot for royalty, was terribly flattered to be the Prince's pal. Unfortunately William also had a fiery temper, and got Horatio tangled up in a dispute about another officer whom he had unfairly sacked.

Cuthbert Collingwood

Collingwood was now Captain of the frigate *Mediator*, but he and Horatio had been friends for some years, having met when they were midshipmen. Cuthbert had gone to sea as an ordinary sailor at the age of 11 and had had to work his way up the ladder of promotion without any help from wealthy relatives. He was promoted to captain because of his bravery in running supplies ashore to British soldiers during the American Revolution. He was

Horatio's opposite in many ways; a big, shy man, very strict with his men, and distant towards his officers. (He preferred the company of his dog, Bounce, who was his companion aboard ship for many years, until it tragically bounced overboard one day.) But although they were so different, Cuthbert and Horatio remained firm friends.

Mary Moutray

Mary Moutray was a dear friend of Collingwood, and Horatio met her through him. She was a pretty, funny, clever woman and both captains fell in love with her – but unfortunately for them she was already married, to Sir Richard Moutray, the Governor of Antigua. Sir Richard was a lot older than his wife, and in poor health, so it wasn't long before he returned to England, taking Mary with him and leaving poor Horatio broken-hearted.

This country appears now intolerable, my dear friend being absent.

But Horatio wasn't the sort of person to mope about for long. He carried on with his campaign against American traders, and captured four ships that disobeyed his order not to anchor at the island of Nevis. This made him so unpopular with the local merchants that they had a whip-round to collect money so that the American ship-

WANTED:

HORATIO NELSON
For being a
BIG GIRLY SPOIL-SPORT
and a
RIGHT PAIN IN THE BEHIND.

owners could take Horatio to court. He was charged with assault and wrongful arrest, and had to stay aboard his ship for two months, afraid that if he set foot ashore he would be carted off to jail.

Eventually the President of Nevis, a man called John Herbert, stepped in and offered to stand bail for Nelson if he wanted to come ashore. Nelson became a regular visitor to his house, Montpelier, a white villa standing high on the slopes of Mount Nevis, with wonderful views of the sea. (The slaves who were forced to work in Mr Herbert's sugar plantation next door probably didn't have a lot of time to enjoy the view, but Horatio, like a lot of Europeans at that time, didn't really see anything wrong with slavery, and he wouldn't have been worried by the fact that John Herbert's beautiful house and posh lifestyle were only made possible by their labour.)

It was at Montpelier that Horatio met Fanny Nisbet, Herbert's niece. She was a widow with a young son and she lived there with her uncle, managing the house for him and looking after his guests. Horatio soon hit it off with her little boy, Josiah. (Mr Herbert once found them playing together under the dining room table.) He also liked Fanny, whom he said reminded him of Mary

Moutray. She wasn't as bright as Mary (some people who knew her thought she was a teeny bit dull) but she was very pretty, and there was a good chance that she would one day inherit some of Mr Herbert's fortune. Horatio decided he was in love, and asked Fanny to marry him.

We may not be a rich couple, yet I have not the least doubt but that we shall be a happy pair – the fault must be mine if we are not.

WHAT, NO WAR?

Horatio and Fanny were married on 11 March 1787, and later that year they returned to England and rented furnished rooms (what we would call a flat) in London. Fanny loved her new hubbie, but she probably wasn't best pleased about the move. After all, where would you rather live…

Answer: a) Correct! Go to the top of the class. b) Sorry, you're just plain WEIRD.

Soon Fanny was complaining that the smoke and fogs of London were damaging her lungs. Meanwhile, Horatio was starting to realize that his behaviour in the West Indies had damaged his chances of another command. His seizure of the American ships and complaints about customs officials had upset a lot of people, and some senior officers seemed to think he was a bit of a troublemaker. With no wars to be fought they were quite happy to let Horatio kick around on shore.

So the happy couple left London and went back to live at Horatio's father's house in Burnham Thorpe. Fanny got on well with old Edmund Nelson, but she thought the house was cold and bleak, and the Norfolk winters were even colder than London. Horatio found it almost as bad.

The Secret Log Book of H. Nelson

8th January 1789

Bored, bored, bored. BORED! The snow has fallen so thick these past three days that the house has been quite cut off. Poor Fanny feels the cold so hard that she spends most of her time in bed, out of the icy drafts. I know how she feels! I have never felt so cold a place as our bedchamber. Wish I could go back to the West Indies, or the Indian Ocean, or anywhere – but

there is precious little hope of a
ship now! Spend my time studying
charts, writing letters to the
Admiralty begging for another ship,
and reading the Norfolk Chronicle
to Father. His eyesight is now so
bad he cannot read the print...
Have told him many times to buy
a pair of spectacles, but he does
not approve of them. He says
failing eyesight is the Lord's will...

10th February

Should I quit England altogether?
I could enter the Russian navy...
or even go to live in France. They
may be foreigners, but at least
they know a brilliant naval hero
when they see one. Wrote a
stiff letter to the Admiralty,
telling them so.

3rd March

NIFTY
RUSSIAN
OUTFIT
→

Bored, bored, bored.
Wrote another stiff
letter to the Admiralty.
Bed.

61

15th April 1789

Fanny complains that there is no social life in Norfolk. She wishes us to remove to Bath or London But what should we live on? I am on half pay, with no prospect of employment, and her rotten uncle has not given her as big an allowance as I had hoped. I do love Fanny, but I wish she wouldn't complain so. Perhaps if we had children things would be different. Young Josiah is all well and good, but I should like children of my own about the place...

6th May

Lately there have been rumours about a war with Spain, so I dashed up to London to see if their lordships would give me a ship.

Saw Lord Hood, a member of the Navy Board, but when I asked him for a job he told me that the King has an unfavourable opinion of me! Apparently His Majesty thinks I was a bad influence on his son, Prince William, and blames me for the mess he got into out in the West Indies. If he wasn't the king I'd say he was a silly old fool...

21st June

Fanny is poorly again; she complains of trouble with her throat and chest, and rheumatism. Wrote to the Admiralty, reminding them that although I am very happily married I am available to sail in the service of my King & country AT ANY TIME. Don't expect a reply of course.

I have been digging a ha-ha (a sort of fashionable ditch) in Father's garden, and planting rose bushes.

At least it gets me out of the house.

HA-HA

Organized a shooting party last week with some of my relations, and shot a partridge, but the others complained at me for firing off my gun without much troubling to take aim.

I told them that if they were so worried about a bit of shot whizzing past their ears they would not be much use boarding an enemy ship, but they would only say 'Yikes!' and 'Watch where you're pointing that thing!' They are a sad bunch of geese.

And so Horatio's boring life in Norfolk dragged on. But across the sea in France, things were about to get very interesting indeed…

THE SOLAR ORB

14th July 1789

FROGS HOPPING MAD!

There were amazing scenes in Paris today! For months the rebellious French peasants and labourers have been moaning on about how unfair it is that they have nothing to eat while the rich aristocrats have all the money and land. Today the grubby grumblers took to the streets and stormed the Bastille prison, where they thought some of their friends were being held.

The revolting rowdies now say they are going to overthrow French King Louis and run France themselves.

The ORB says: Pull the other one, Monsewer Pongy-pants!

News of the revolution in France raced across Europe. It was the biggest thing to happen for years, and people reacted in lots of different ways. Many were glad to see that the old order of kings and aristocrats was being challenged at last. But a lot of rich landowners in Britain were thinking:

> OOH ER! IF IT CAN HAPPEN IN FRANCE, IT COULD HAPPEN HERE TOO!

And some of the labourers who worked on their land were thinking,

> OOH ARR! IF IT CAN HAPPEN IN FRANCE, IT COULD HAPPEN HERE TOO!

There were soon reports of trouble all over the country. Members of radical societies went from pub to pub, stirring up talk about revolution and encouraging poor people to stop paying taxes.

Horatio was horrified. He believed in a well-ordered society with the king at the top and the poor firmly in their place at the bottom. But at the same time he believed in treating people fairly, and he could see why the people were unhappy.

In a letter to his pal Prince William he wrote:

It is little wonder that they have been seduced by promises of better times, for they are really in want of everything to make life comfortable. It is the fault of the country gentlemen, who have not made their farmers raise their wages as the cost of food etc. increased. Their wages have been raised within these three weeks by a shilling a week; had it been done before they would not have been discontented, for a want of loyalty is not among their faults.

The discontent rumbled on and on, but it never flared up into open revolution. Meanwhile, across the Channel, things were going from bad to worse.

THE SOLAR ORB

20th June 1791

KING CAPTURED!

The rotten revolutionary government now ruling France has announced that King Louis has been captured whilst trying to escape the country, cunningly disguised as an escaping king. He will be taken back to Paris to stand trial!

The ORB says: IT'S AN OUTRAGE! Kings should be treated with respect, even if they are only foreigners!

28th February 1792

FROG NOBS' NODDLES NOBBLED BY NEW-FANGLED NOGGIN KNOCKER-OFFER

They're calling it 'The Terror'. Every day in Paris the evil revolutionaries are beheading hundreds of innocent aristocrats on a new bonce-chopping machine called a 'Guillotine'! The latest rumours say that King Louis himself will be for the chop when he's been tried. But never fear! The other royal families of Europe won't allow this sort of thing to carry on for much longer: Austria and Prussia have formed an alliance to stamp out the revolution and restore King Louis to his rightful place on the throne!

The ORB says: About time too! This revolutionary rabble will never be able to stand up to a REAL army!

21st September 1792

PRUSSIANS RUSHIN' FOR COVER!

The King of Prussia's well-trained army has been chased back out of France by the soldiers of the revolutionary government after their surprise defeat yesterday at the Battle of Valmy. It seems the French are keener to defend their new-found freedom than anybody expected. Meanwhile in Paris, the terror continues, with innocent men and women losing their heads just for being from old aristocratic families.

The ORB says: It's time we sorted these foreign types out! Britain must act!

Sure enough, preparations for war were soon underway in Britain. The Brits hadn't wanted to get involved at first, but now that their revolution had been such a success at home it seemed the French were planning to take it on tour and start invading neighbouring countries. In 1793 a small squadron of British ships was sent to see what was going on in the French naval bases on the other side of the Channel. One of them was fired on by French guns as it cruised outside the harbour at Brest.

Three weeks later orders came for Horatio to go aboard his new ship, the *Agamemnon*. He could hardly wait, and set about recruiting a crew for her at once. Unfortunately, Fanny couldn't share his excitement. She was upset at the thought that he would soon be going to sea, and worried about what might happen to him when he fought the French.

NIPPING OFF TO NAPLES

The *Agamemnon* set sail for the Mediterranean, where she was to join a British fleet on patrol off the south coast of France. On the way she stopped off at Cadiz in Spain (the Brits and the Spanish were at peace, for once). There, Horatio saw his first bullfight – and also his last, since he didn't enjoy it very much. For somebody whose job involved fighting bloody battles, he could be surprisingly squeamish.

It ... turned us sick and we could hardly sit it out. The dead, mangled horses with their entrails tore out, the bulls covered with blood, was too much. However, we have seen one, and agree that nothing shall tempt us to see another.

Then it was on into the Mediterranean, where Admiral Lord Hood's fleet was cruising to and fro outside the ports of Marseilles and Toulon to make sure no French warships got out.

The Secret Log Book of H. Nelson

2nd August 1793

We have been cruising off Toulon for about a month now. It's good to be back at sea, but I wish there was more interesting business at hand. We are starting to run low on fresh food, so all we "get" for our trouble is honour and salt beef. But I daresay it is worse ashore. The master of a merchant ship from Marseilles told us that the people of France "are starving and live in terror of their cruel revolutionary government.

I've heard that the French navy have been fitting their ships with furnaces so that they can fire red-hot cannon balls" at us and start fires aboard "our ships. Well, if we go into battle I shall take Agamemnon "so close that their shots go through one "side and out the other and it shall not matter if they are hot or cold! &

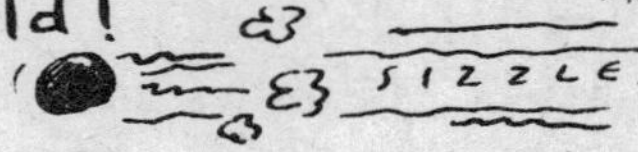

& SIZZLE!

28th August 1793

Amazing news! Toulon has surrendered to us, without so much as a shot being fired! It seems the people there are tired of revolution. They have declared loyalty to the French royal family and have invited our fleet to enter their great harbour. Marseilles tried to surrender too, but the revolutionary army got there too fast for us and occupied it, killing hundreds of people. Luckily, Toulon is heavily fortified. But if we are to hold off the revolutionaries we will need a garrison of at least 50,000 men – and that's bigger than the entire British army!

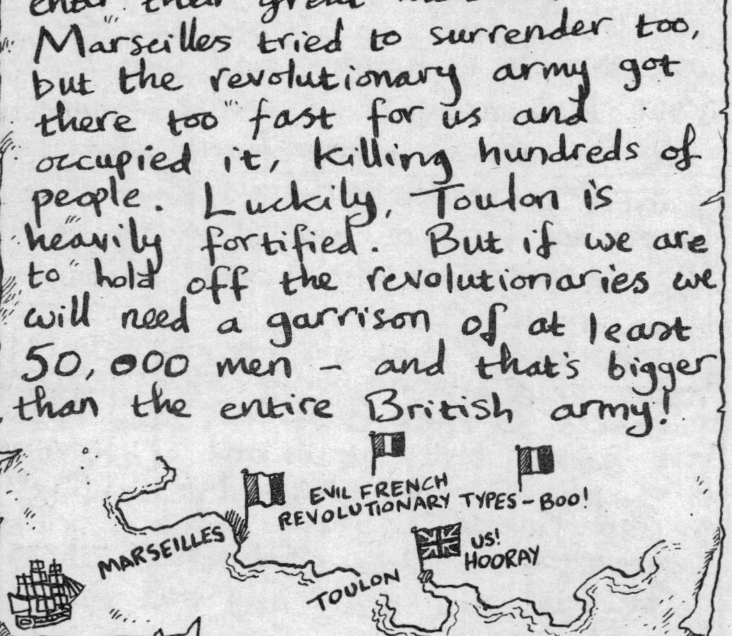

EVIL FRENCH REVOLUTIONARY TYPES – BOO!

MARSEILLES

TOULON

US! HOORAY

4th September 1793

Boo! I'm not to go into Toulon after all! I shall be very upset if I miss a good battle! Instead, Lord Hood is sending me east to Naples. The king there is a relative of poor king Louis, and married to Maria Carolina, sister of French queen Marie Antoinette, whom those dastardly revolutionaries have imprisoned! Lord Hood hopes I can persuade them to send soldiers to help defend Toulon.

Kings and things

In Nelson's day Italy was still made up of lots of different independent states and kingdoms. The Kingdom of the Two Sicilies covered the island of Sicily and the mainland south of Rome. Confused? I know I am, so here's a map:

LIVORNO – A NEUTRAL PORT, WHICH THE BRITS CALLED 'LEGHORN'.

THESE BITS ARE OWNED BY THE AUSTRIAN EMPIRE...

PAPAL STATES

THE KINGDOM OF THE TWO SICILIES

TOULON

CORSICA

•ROME

NAPLES

SARDINIA

PALERMO

SICILY

N

And here's a nice picture of the Sicilian king and queen...

King Ferdinand was a member of the powerful Bourbon family, who were so important that they provided kings for France and Spain too, and had a very nice biscuit named after them. His favourite hobbies were hunting wild animals (which he shot from the safety of a sentrybox while his servants drove them into range) and fishing. He cooked and sold his catches at his own fried-fish stall. Educated, middle-class people in Naples couldn't stand him – but the poor people thought he was great.

Queen Maria Carolina was much more intelligent than her husband. It was Maria who kept the state running while her hubby was out selling his fish. She was also very religious, and had a habit of scribbling prayers on bits of paper which she then stuffed inside her clothes, or ate. She had 18 children, only eight of whom were still alive when Nelson arrived.

Ferdy and Maria held court in the city of Naples, and it was there that Horatio went with his request for reinforcements. The city stood on the beautiful Bay of Naples, famous for the volcano Mount Vesuvius, and also for the Roman city of Pompeii which had been buried by an eruption in AD 79 and was just starting to be excavated in Nelson's time. But although Naples was a place that every tasteful tourist just had to see, much of the city consisted of smelly slums. One English visitor reported:

Children relieve themselves whenever they feel the urge, and even people in carriages often get out to mix with the pedestrians for the same purpose.

The city was also famous for its pickpockets and layabouts, but King Ferdy did nothing about them because most of them were fierce royalists. It was the poor, along with the Catholic Church, who kept him in power.

Hanging out with the Hamiltons

As soon as he went ashore in Naples, Horatio went to find the British ambassador Sir William Hamilton. Sir William was a fanatical collector of paintings and ancient artefacts, especially Greek and Roman vases, and was something of an expert on volcanoes – he often climbed Mount Vesuvius to peek into its crater, sometimes in the middle of an eruption. He had lived in Naples for more than 20 years and was a great friend of the King and Queen, whom he soon persuaded to send 2,000 Sicilian soldiers to help defend Toulon.

He also had a beautiful young wife named Emma. Horatio barely met her on this first visit, but she would one day become the most important person in his life, so while our hero sails back to Toulon with the reinforcements, let's take a break and look at...

The Emma Hamilton Story

EMMA WAS THE DAUGHTER OF A CHESHIRE BLACKSMITH, BUT HER FATHER DIED WHEN SHE WAS ONLY TWO MONTHS OLD AND SHE WAS SENT TO LIVE WITH HER GRANNY IN WALES.

WHAT A DUMP!

BAA!
BAA!

AT THE AGE OF 12 SHE STARTED WORK AS A HOUSEMAID FOR A COMPOSER CALLED WILLIAM LINLEY...

WHEN SHE WAS 16 SHE CAUGHT THE EYE OF ONE OF LINLEY'S RICH CHUMS, SIR HARRY FETHERSTONEHAUGH (PRONOUNCED 'FANSHAW').

SHE WENT TO LIVE ON SIR HARRY'S ESTATE IN SUSSEX, WHERE SHE HAD HIS BABY, A GIRL NAMED EMMA.

PHWETHERSTONEHAUGH! (PRONOUNCED 'PHWOOAR!')

BUT SIR HARRY GREW TIRED OF EMMA AND PASSED HER ON TO HIS FRIEND CHARLES GREVILLE, WHO HAD EXPENSIVE TASTES BUT NOT MUCH MONEY.

I SAY! YOU'RE A BIT OF ALL RIGHT!

I'LL GET THAT FAMOUS ARTIST CHAPPIE ROMNEY TO RUN UP SOME PICS OF YOU, THEN FLOG 'EM FOR A TIDY PROFIT!

AFTER LIVING WITH EMMA FOR A FEW YEARS, GREVILLE DECIDED THAT HE WANTED TO GET MARRIED — TO SOMEBODY ELSE.

EMMA'S ALL VERY WELL, BUT MISS MIDDLETON'S FROM A GOOD FAMILY — AND SHE'S HEIR TO HER DAD'S FORTUNE! BUT WHAT ON EARTH SHALL I DO WITH EMMA?

77

GOT IT! I'LL INTRODUCE HER TO MY UNCLE, SIR WILLIAM HAMILTON. HE COULD DO WITH A PRETTY GIRLFRIEND NOW HIS WIFE'S DEAD – AND HE MIGHT BE SO GRATEFUL THAT HE'LL LEAVE ME ALL HIS MONEY!

SO EMMA WAS PACKED OFF TO STAY WITH SIR WILLIAM IN NAPLES, NOT REALIZING THAT GREVILLE WAS DUMPING HER...

HAVE A NICE HOLIDAY, DEAR!

HEH HEH! THAT'S THE LAST I'LL SEE OF HER!

AFTER A COUPLE OF MONTHS AT SIR WILLIAM'S BEAUTIFUL VILLA, THE PALAZZO SESSA, EMMA REALIZED THAT GREVILLE DIDN'T WANT HER BACK.

BOO HOO!

BUT BY THAT TIME, SIR WILLIAM HAD FALLEN IN LOVE WITH HER.

YOU'RE JUST WHAT I NEED TO COMPLETE MY COLLECTION!

IN 1791 THEY WERE MARRIED.

POO!

THE TIMES

The Hamiltons made an unlikely couple. Sir William was old, posh and rather reserved. Emma was less than half his age, boisterous and friendly. (She was also a bit on the plump side, but you didn't have to be a beanpole to be beautiful in the 18th century.) Anyway, Sir William loved her. He didn't mind that her manners weren't up to much, or that her spelling was atroshus. He didn't even mind when her mum came to live with them. (Somewhere along the way Emma had managed to abandon her own daughter – a child would probably have cramped her style.) Anyway, Sir William liked having beautiful things about him, and he was very proud to show off his glamourous young wife.

The house is full of painters painting me. There is another man modelling me in wax and another in clay. All the artists is come from Rome to study me. Sir William says he loves nothing but me.

And Emma wasn't just a pretty face. She soon made great friends with Queen Maria, which was useful to Sir William when he wanted influence at the court. She also became famous for her 'Attitudes', which she performed to impress visitors to the Palazzo Sessa. They involved her posing like a sort of human statue.

How to impress your friends, the Emma Hamilton way

1. Stand behind a large picture frame. If you don't have a picture frame, two curtains will do.
2. Imagine you are a character from ancient history or mythology – the more tragic, the better.

> I SHALL NOW PORTRAY QUEEN DIDO, PINING FOR HER LOVER AENEAS...

3. Stand very still.
4. Keep on standing still.
5. Stand still a bit longer.
6. Curtsey to wild applause, then strike another Attitude.

> I SHALL NOW BE HELEN OF TROY.

You might think that watching somebody stand still would be about as exciting as sitting through your uncle Albert's holiday slides of Rhyll, but Sir William's guests lapped up Emma's performances. The famous German writer Goethe, who stayed at the Palazzo Sessa in 1787, said: 'She gives so much variety to her poses, gestures, expressions etc. that the spectator can hardly believe his eyes.'

This proves that either people were much more easily impressed in the 18th century, or Emma was a very good actress. It also proves that, when your gran tells you what fun it was in the old days when we didn't have TV and people made their own entertainment, SHE IS WRONG!

SO LONG, TOULON

In the end, the British defence of Toulon didn't last long. Even with the reinforcements that Horatio brought back from Naples, the French revolutionary armies were soon able to capture the outer parts of the city. Before long the British ships in the harbour were being hammered by French cannons commanded by a brilliant young officer.

BOOM!

YES, FANS, IT IS I, NAPOLEON BONAPARTE, ZE FUTURE EMPEREUR OF FRANCE!

But more about him later.

Finally, on 17th December 1793, the British left. Fifteen thousand townspeople were able to escape with them, but the rest were left behind to face the angry revolutionaries.

Now the Brits needed a new base in the Mediterranean. They decided to try and capture the island of Corsica, which was already in revolt against the French, and Horatio was busy with battles and sieges on the island through much of 1794. Once, while he was watching the bombardment of the French fortress of Calvi, an enemy shell exploded among some sandbags just in front of him, spraying him with sand and stones. He was not badly wounded, but his face was cut and bruised and his right eye was damaged. Three weeks later he wrote home to Fanny:

> *My eye is as far recovered as to be able to distinguish light from darkness, but as to all the purpose of use it is gone.*

Back in Norfolk, Fanny was beside herself with worry at the thought that Horatio and Josiah were risking their lives. She didn't understand that her husband was having the time of his life. He would probably have liked her to write him letters that went...

MY DEAREST HUSBAND, GOSH, AREN'T YOU AMAZINGLY BRAVE AND WONDERFUL! I'M SO PROUD TO BE MARRIED TO THE GREATEST HERO IN THE WHOLE WORLD EVER! WHO CARES IF YOU'VE LOST AN EYE? YOU'VE GOT A SPARE ONE!

Instead, she wrote things like this:

Fanny's worries weren't the only things that were getting on his nerves. When Corsica finally surrendered he didn't get as much credit for the victory as he thought he deserved. Then, early in 1795, Lord Hood went home to England and a new admiral took command of the Mediterranean fleet. Vice Admiral Hotham was a cautious man, not at all like Horatio, and Horatio was furious when he twice let enemy fleets escape rather than risk a battle in the dangerous waters near the French coast. He was sure that he could have made a better job of it, and modestly declared: 'had I commanded our Fleet … either the whole French Fleet should have graced my triumph or I should have been in a confounded scrape!'

But later that year Hotham was replaced by Sir John Jervis, a fiery old admiral who knew and liked Horatio and quickly promoted him to commodore. This was a temporary rank which meant that he was in charge of a whole squadron of ships instead of just his own new ship, the *Captain*. It also meant that he got paid an extra ten shillings a day.

Things were starting to look up a bit, and Horatio hoped that soon he'd have the chance for glory that he'd been waiting for for so long.

Meanwhile in Paris...

Remember those repellent revolutionaries? They were still busy beheading people. King Louis went to the guillotine, and so did Queen Marie Antoinette and the rest of the royal family. Then, when they'd run out of aristocrats, the revolutionaries started on each other.

At last Citizen Robespierre, top noggin-chopper and head of the revolutionary government, had his own head chopped off. He was replaced by the Directory, a five-man group who took over the business of ruling France.

Luckily for them, they did.

MOI AGAIN, FANS! YES, I WAS SO FANTASTIQUE AT ZE SIEGE OF TOULON ZAT ZE DIRECTORY 'AS PUT ME IN CHARGE OF ZE 'OLE ARMY FOR ZIS NEW CAMPAIGN! WATCH OUT, SPAGHETTI-SCOFFING ITALIAN-TYPE PIPPLE — 'ERE I CURM!

Sure enough, nifty Napoleon caught the Austrians napping, and the invasion of Italy was a huge success. By April 1795 he'd captured Milan. The rest of Italy was so alarmed that the British fleet soon found it hard to find a port anywhere in the country: Leghorn had been grabbed by the French; Genoa was so keen not to upset nasty Napoleon that it fired at any British ship that came near; and there was even trouble in Naples, where King Ferdinand's enemies were talking about booting him out and setting up a republic.

Worse still, the Spanish saw which way the wind was blowing and sided with the French. Since Holland and Prussia had also been forced to make peace with France, the Brits were left more or less alone. In 1796 the British Government decided that its fleet couldn't stay in the Mediterranean now that France and Spain were both against it, and the ships were ordered home. Nelson was appalled…

> BUT OUR FLEET COULD EASILY BEAT THAT BUNCH OF FOREIGNERS, EVEN IF WE ARE COMPLETELY OUTNUMBERED!

Still, there was nothing he could do about it, so he started for home. But his ship was delayed looking for a man who had fallen overboard, and when he sailed on, he ran into thick fog.

Nelson's frigate pulled away fast and caught up with the rest of the British fleet off Cape St Vincent in southern Portugal. When Horatio reported what he had seen, Admiral Jervis immediately turned his ships around to meet the Spanish. All through that night they steered towards the sound of the Spaniards' signal-guns, and at dawn on the following day the huge shapes of Spanish warships loomed out of the mist. The captain of Admiral Jervis's flagship started to get worried.

THERE ARE EIGHT SAIL-OF-THE-LINE, SIR JOHN.

VERY WELL.

THERE ARE 20 SAIL-OF-THE-LINE, SIR JOHN.

VERY WELL

THERE ARE 27 SAIL-OF-THE-LINE, SIR JOHN— AND WE'VE ONLY GOT 16!

ENOUGH, SIR! THE DIE IS CAST AND IF THERE ARE 50 SAIL I WILL GO THROUGH THEM. ENGLAND BADLY NEEDS A VICTORY AT PRESENT.

ALL AT SEA : BLOODY BATTLES

The point of a sea battle in Nelson's time wasn't to sink the enemy's ships. It was very difficult to sink a wooden warship (unless a lucky shot started a fire in her gunpowder store, or you drove her on to a rock). It was also very silly. Warships were slow to build and cost a fortune, so a captured enemy ship was much more valuable than one at the bottom of the sea – the Royal Navy was full of French-built warships that had been captured in earlier fights. (Horatio's first ship, the *Raisonnable* was one of them.)

As the ships sailed into battle, the decks would be cleared of anything not needed in the fighting. Hammocks were brought up from below and hung in the rigging to shield the men on deck from flying splinters, and the carpenter and his mates quickly removed the partitions in the captain's cabin to make room for guns. 'Fear-nought' screens were placed over the hatchways leading to the lower decks, in case any scaredy-cat sailors tried to scurry out of harm's way, and wet canvas curtains were hung at the entrances to the powder-store to prevent sparks getting in there.

Meanwhile, a marine beat his drum to warn everyone to get to their correct 'quarters'. The captain took his place on the quarterdeck, while marine sharpshooters climbed into the 'tops' – platforms high up on the masts, from where they could fire down on to an enemy's deck. The boatswain and his mates stood ready to repair any damage to sails and rigging. An important rope shot away in the middle of a battle could make a ship unmanageable and mean the difference between victory and defeat.

The rest of the men ran to man the guns, with a lieutenant in command of each side of each gundeck. To do maximum damage, the guns on each side of the ship fired all together in a 'broadside'. The Brits were generally better trained in gunnery than the French or Spanish, and that training could make all the difference in battle. Each gun needed a crew of at least six.

THE GUN IS LOADED WITH GUNPOWDER AND SHOT.

THE CREW HAUL THE GUN TO THE GUNPORT AND THE GUN CAPTAIN TAKES AIM.

HANDSPIKES ARE USED TO RAISE OR LOWER THE BARREL

THE 'POWDER MONKEY'—OFTEN JUST A YOUNG BOY— RUNS TO AND FRO FETCHING SUPPLIES OF GUNPOWDER FROM THE STORES.

THE GUN CAPTAIN FIRES THE GUN, AND EVERYONE STANDS CLEAR AS IT RECOILS.

THE CREW PREPARE TO DAMP DOWN SPARKS AND RE-LOAD.

The guns didn't just fire cannon balls. **Bar** or **chain-shot** was used to tear through sails and rigging and smash masts. **Grapeshot** was like a party pack of small cannon balls wrapped in a canvas bag. **Canister shot** consisted of hundreds of small steel balls, in a case that would burst when fired, killing or wounding anyone in its path. As if it wasn't dangerous enough to have all that flying around there were also splinters of wood, often huge and heavy and very, very sharp. These might be torn from the ship's hull and upper works as enemy shot thudded into it, and often killed and injured as many sailors as the actual gunfire. And when all else failed, a crew might have to **board** the enemy ship, fighting hand to hand with cutlasses, pikes, pistols and axes. Finally, when a ship could fight no more, her surviving officers would haul down her flag and surrender.

It's no wonder that, every time a battle loomed, Horatio thought that he was probably about to die…

Secret Log Book of H Nelson

14th February 1797
♥ Valentine's day! ♥

What a day! And what a battle!

I don't mind admitting I was nervous as we sailed towards the Spanish fleet this morning! Those Spanish ships are real thumpers! One of the other captains said they looked like the cliffs of Beachy Head as they loomed out of the mist, sails set, heading for Cadiz. I reminded myself that this was the moment I'd been waiting for: in another few hours I'd either be dead or a hero!

We soon realized that they were sailing in two loose formations. The admiral ordered us to form a line and steer between them, then turn and attack the two groups one at a time. But my ship was near the back of the line, and as we approached I could see that the Spanish formations were joining up. I knew that Sir John's plan could only work if the gap between the two groups stayed open,

So I decided to bring them to battle straight away. I broke formation and steered into the midst of seven Spanish warships. I will say something for the Spaniards – they certainly know how to build! Their ships are huge, and one, the Santisima Trinidad, is the largest warship in the world! But although they build them well, they ain't so good at fighting as our sailors, and their gun crews can't aim so true or fire so quick as ours. Which was lucky for us, as pretty soon things got very warm indeed, with shot and splinters howling across the decks and the sharpshooters' muskets crackling in the tops.

By the time some other of our ships came to help, we had been so shot about that my people thought we would have to bow out and leave the fighting to others. Well, I wasn't having that! I ordered my crew to ram the nearest Spaniard, the San Nicholas. As we crashed against her I drew my sword and called for boarders. Lieutenant Berry leapt into the Spaniard's mizzen-chains, and a marine smashed one of the windows in her stern-gallery and jumped through, followed by myself and my men behind me all huzza-ing and halloo-ing and waving cutlasses and boarding pikes. We fought our way up through smoke and chaos and confusion onto their quarterdeck, where I found the Spaniards already hauling down

their flag to show that they had surrendered.

But just as we were starting to congratulate ourselves upon our victory, we were fired upon with pistols and muskets from another ship, the San Josef, that had somehow got its rigging entangled with the San Nicholas's in the heat of battle (rotten seamen, these foreigners). Quick as a flash, I decided to capture her as well! As soon as I was sure that we had the San Nicholas secure I called again for boarders, and as I got into the San Josef's main-chains a Spanish officer came up to me and said that the ship had surrendered! Later the Spanish captain presented his sword to me on bended knee!!

CAPTAIN — SAN NICHOLAS — SAN JOSEF

We had captured one enemy, and crossed her to board and take a second, which is something never seen before and most amazing heroic!

Hurrah for me!

Meanwhile, the rest of the British fleet were making short work of the other Spanish ships. The Battle of Cape St Vincent was a huge victory, and at last Horatio had some of the recognition he had always wanted. He was made a Knight of the Order of the Bath, and a week after the battle he heard that he had been promoted to rear admiral.

ALL AT SEA: ADMIRABLE ADMIRALS

Being a rear admiral wasn't the top job in the Navy – vice admirals were more important, and even they had to take orders from full admirals – but it was still pretty good going for a 39-year-old rector's son from Norfolk. His new rank meant that Horatio would be put in charge of whole fleets of ships, or at least large parts of them. His headquarters would be aboard his 'flagship'. Of course, with battles to plan and all those other vessels to think about, he wasn't expected to be responsible for the day-to-day running of his own ship any more; he had someone called a 'flag captain' to take care of that.

Almost as important to Horatio as his promotion was the fact that everyone in England now knew his name and how he had captured the two Spanish ships. Fanny had been spending the winter in Bath, along with Edmund Nelson, and they found that complete strangers were all talking about the battle and stopping them in the street to congratulate them on Horatio's part in it.

But Fanny was still worried about him… Soon after the battle she wrote: 'What can I attempt to say to you about boarding? You have done desperate actions enough. I beg that you never board again. Leave it to captains.'

ARMLESS HORATIO

Poor Fanny might as well have been writing to a brick wall. Almost as soon as her letter reached him, Horatio was in the thick of the fighting again. This time he left the safety of his new flagship, the *Theseus*, to lead a flotilla of small boats in a night attack on Cadiz harbour. An admiral wouldn't usually get involved in risky operations of this sort, but Nelson was keen to show his sailors that he was prepared to fight and die alongside them – especially since the Royal Navy was suddenly full of discontent and talk of mutiny.

ALL AT SEA : MURDEROUS MUTINIES

A mutiny was a sort of ship-board revolution, which happened when a crew finally got fed up with a cruel or over-strict captain. The first sign of trouble was often **shot-rolling**, when grumpy sailors on the night-watch would roll cannon balls along the deck in the dark. The rolling shot might knock an unwary officer off his feet, and the grumbling sound of the trundling cannon balls would make the rest of the crew aware that mutiny was afoot.

Sometimes the mutineers were able to persuade the ship's marines, and even some of the officers, to join them in an attempt to take over the ship. If that happened, the captain and his supporters might be in real trouble – like cruel Captain Bligh, who was cast adrift in an open boat with a few loyal sailors when mutineers took over his ship, the *Bounty* in 1789. (Actually, beastly Bligh was all right in the end. He was a fantastic navigator, and managed to steer his little boat to safety.)

Not surprisingly, the Royal Navy took a dim view of this sort of thing, and did everything it could to stop it happening. Men found guilty of mutiny were hung, and discontented crews were split up and sent to other ships.

A lot of the Navy's seamen were sick and tired of low pay. In 1797 the trouble came to a head. The crews of ships anchored at Spithead, near the important naval base of Portsmouth, went on strike and demanded better conditions. To everyone's surprise, the Admiralty gave in to them, but before long there was another more serious mutiny among the ships stationed off Chatham at the Nore. This time the Admiralty took a tougher line. They blamed the sailors' complaints on 'Jacobins' – supporters of the ideas of the French Revolution. The mutiny was crushed by force, and the ringleaders hanged – but it took the Brits a long time to get over the shock of having their own fleet rebel against them.

Nelson hated the whole idea of mutiny, just as he hated the idea of revolution. But he did understand the conditions that sometimes drove men to it, and sympathized with them. Although he said he would be 'happy to command a ship' against 'the Nore scoundrels', he also said that seamen were 'a neglected set' and 'when peace comes, shamefully treated'. He did his best to look into any complaints they made, and sometimes took their side against over-strict officers. In 1797 the men of the *Blanche*, one of the frigates in his squadron, refused to sail under a new captain who had a reputation as a fierce disciplinarian. Another British officer told them:

Now, my lads, if you resist taking Captain Hotham as your captain, every third man shall be hung.

The crew grabbed guns and crowbars and for a while it looked as if a mutiny was certain. Then Horatio came aboard, gathered them round him and said:

> *Lads, you have the greatest character of any frigate crew in the Navy… If Captain Hotham treats you ill, give me a letter and I will support you.*

THREE CHEERS FOR ADMIRAL NELSON!

On his own ship, Horatio always tried to make sure that the men were happy, and while he wasn't afraid to flog or even hang men when he thought it was necessary, he often tried to find less severe punishments. The men seem to have appreciated it. Around the time of the fight at Cadiz, this anonymous note was dropped on the quarterdeck of the *Theseus* one night.

SUCCESS ATTEND ADMIRAL NELSON! GOD BLESS CAPTAIN MILLER! WE THANK THEM FOR THE OFFICERS THEY HAVE PLACED OVER US. WE ARE HAPPY AND COMFORTABLE AND WILL SHED EVERY DROP OF BLOOD IN OUR VEINS TO SUPPORT THEM, AND THE NAME OF THE THESEUS WILL BE IMMORTALIZED AS HIGH AS THE CAPTAIN'S.
FROM THE SHIP'S COMPANY.

Trouble at Tenerife

A month after the fight at Cadiz, Horatio was back in action again, this time leading a squadron sent to attack Tenerife in the Canary Islands. These days the islands are famous for sea, sand and sunburn and the only people who invade them are holidaymakers, but in 1797 Tenerife's main port of Santa Cruz was still an important stopping place for Spanish treasure galleons on their way home from the gold and silver mines of the New World. Two such ships were believed to be anchored in Santa Cruz when Nelson was sent there. The thought of all that prize money is probably one reason why the Brits were so keen to capture the island.

The plan was that the Brits would anchor out of sight of the islands and make a surprise attack by night in small boats. But the first attack, led by Captain Troubridge, was foiled by bad weather and strong currents. The next night Horatio decided to lead the boats in himself – even though he knew the Spanish would be ready for them. Josiah – who had served with him ever since leaving Norfolk, and was now a lieutenant – volunteered to go with him...

It was a good thing for Horatio that he did. The Brits came under heavy fire as their boats drew near the shore, and Horatio was hit in the right elbow by a musket ball and fell back into the boat, saying, 'I'm a dead man!'

Josiah quickly took charge. He clapped his hat over the wound to hide the blood (the sight of it was making Nelson feel faint), then took off his neckcloth to make a tourniquet, while another sailor ripped up his shirt for a sling. Then he ordered the boat's crew to row back as fast as they could to the waiting ships.

But although Horatio was badly wounded, he wasn't going to stop being a hero. As the boat pulled away from the shore he saw that the water was full of struggling sailors from another boat that had been sunk, and ordered his men to stop and pick them up. It was half an hour before they reached the nearest British ship, the *Seahorse*, and when they did, Horatio refused to let them take him aboard. The *Seahorse*'s captain had gone ashore with the others, but his wife was on board, and Horatio said:

I would rather die than alarm Mrs Fremantle by her seeing me in this state, when I can give her no tidings whatever of her husband.

The oarsmen pulled as hard as they could for the *Theseus*, and when they reached it Horatio insisted on going up the side alone. He told the ship's surgeon to get his instruments ready to amputate the wounded arm.

The sooner it is off, the better.

Down in the dimly-lit medical bay, deep below the water line, the ship's surgeon set to work with his saws and scalpels. The operation was performed without anaesthetic, and later Horatio claimed that the cold knife cutting his flesh was the worst part, much more painful than the sawing through of the bone. Afterwards he gave an order that surgeons must always heat their knives before an operation.

Meanwhile, the battle on shore was ending in disaster. Most of the boats had been swept past the landing site or smashed to pieces in the surf. Some men managed to get ashore, and fighting went on for most of the night, but the Brits were badly outnumbered. Just after sunrise they manged to agree a deal with the Spanish commander...

If you promise never to attack the Canary Islands again you will be allowed to keep your weapons and return to your ships. We will even let you take on fresh water and provisions before you go.

Which was very nice of him, wasn't it?

Horatio's attack on Tenerife had been a catastrophic failure. One hundred and fifty three men had been killed, and it was mainly Horatio's fault; he had got used to winning, and had underestimated the Spanish. He became very depressed and self-pitying…

A left-handed admiral will never again be considered useful, therefore the sooner I get to a very humble cottage the better and make room for a better man to serve the state.

But Admiral Jervis (who had now become Lord St Vincent, in honour of his victory there) refused to blame Horatio for the fiasco and sent him home to recover from his wound, promising that he would have another command as soon as he was ready.

As for the arm, it was buried at sea, sewn up in a hammock with a dead sailor.

FOILING THE FRENCH

All the way back to England Horatio fretted about what sort of welcome he would get. Would people remember him as the man who had captured two Spanish men-o'-war at Cape St Vincent? Or as a great big fool who led his men to disaster at Santa Cruz?

He needn't have worried. There was so much bad news around, what with the mutiny at the Nore and Napoleon still rampaging through Europe, that the Brits badly needed a hero, and they thought Horatio was just the man for the job. He was cheered in the streets and had an audience with the king, and prints of his portrait sold like hot cakes.

TWO HOT CAKES AND A PORTRAIT OF NELSON, PLEASE.

There were even Nelson ballads, including this one about his exploits at Cape St Vincent:

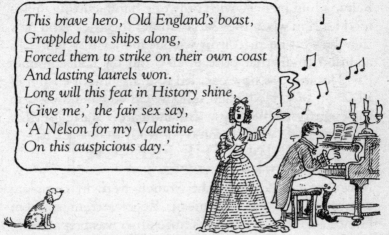

This brave hero, Old England's boast,
Grappled two ships along,
Forced them to strike on their own coast
And lasting laurels won.
Long will this feat in History shine,
'Give me,' the fair sex say,
'A Nelson for my Valentine
On this auspicious day.'

As for the Tenerife business, people just put it down to bad luck.

All this fame and adulation helped Horatio cheer up, but his wounded arm took longer to heal. The stump went septic, and poor Fanny had the job of cleaning it and changing his bandages, while doctor after doctor came to tut tut and say:

WE MUST LEAVE IT TO TIME AND NATURE TO HEAL.

Oddly enough, this turned out to be one of the happiest periods that Fanny and Horatio spent together.

She might not have been much good at being a hero's wife, but she enjoyed nursing him back to health and helping him manage with only one hand, cutting up his food for him when they sat at dinner together. And now they had no need to worry about money any more. In addition to all that prize money and his rear admiral's pay, Horatio was now entitled to a disability pension of £1,000 a year. He bought a house called Roundwood in the countryside near Ipswich, and Fanny started setting up home there while Horatio got ready to go back to sea.

Back to work

It was now 1798, and the French were in complete control of the Mediterranean. Reports from spies in France said that Napoleon's huge army was preparing to embark from Toulon and Marseilles, accompanied by a large fleet of warships. The trouble was, nobody seemed to know where he was planning to take them. Was he going to invade Portugal? Or the Kingdom of the Two Sicilies? Or did he mean to sail round into the Atlantic and land in Ireland, to help Irish rebels there kick out the Brits?

PAH! WHY SHOULD I TELL YOU? YOU ARE ONLY ZE PATHETIC TINY-BRAINED DEAD FAMURSE READING TYPES. I AM A **GENIUS**. (ZAT IS WHY I WEAR ZIS ENORMURSE HAT.)

Horatio's task would be to find out where Nap was off to – and try to stop him.

Secret Log Book of H Nelson

oops - can't get used
to writing with my
left hand like
this...

20th May 1798
At Sea off Toulon

Hurrah for me again! Not only
have I brought a British squadron
back into the Med for the first time
in ages, I even stopped to capture
a French ship on the way! The
prisoners tell me that Napoleon's
army is about to set sail, accompanied
by 15 sail-of-the-line under Admiral
~~Brey~~ Brewys. Unfortunately they
don't know where he is planning
to go. Not to worry. I've brought my
squadron so close to Toulon that I
can see the masts of the French
fleet in the harbour. They certainly
look as if they're getting ready to
sail in the next few days. All we
have to do is watch and wait.

(Note: Captain Berry says the
weather is on the turn...)

24th May 1798

Disaster! There I was on Sunday evening, crowing about my success. Now my squadron is scattered, my ship is dismasted and I couldn't fight off a single French frigate, let alone a fleet.

A tempest of wind struck at about midnight Sunday, and Berry was too slow in furling our sails. All our masts were blown down, one after the next, killing two topsail hands. Luckily we hacked the wreckage free before it smashed in our sides, and one of the other ships towed us away from the shore, where we should otherwise have been dashed into pieces!

For four days since, all hands have been hard at work repairing the damage and we are now seaworthy again. But while our ships were scattered, the French fleet came out of Toulon and passed us in the dark. Now they are gone, and we do not know where...

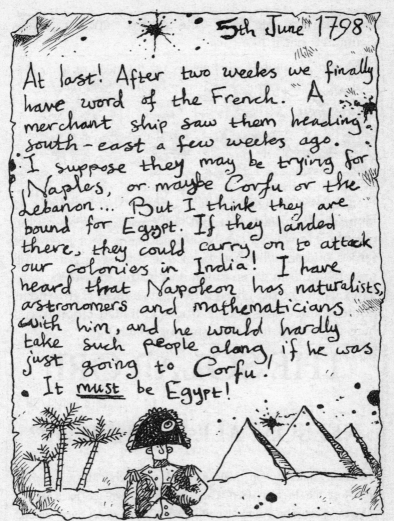

5th June 1798

At last! After two weeks we finally have word of the French. A merchant ship saw them heading south-east a few weeks ago. I suppose they may be trying for Naples, or maybe Corfu or the Lebanon... But I think they are bound for Egypt. If they landed there, they could carry on to attack our colonies in India! I have heard that Napoleon has naturalists, astronomers and mathematicians with him, and he would hardly take such people along, if he was just going to Corfu! It _must_ be Egypt!

By this time Horatio's squadron had been strengthened by the arrival of ten more 74-gun ships, and he ordered them to set sail at once for Egypt, in the hope that he would find the French fleet anchored at Alexandria. He was taking a big risk. One of his captains, James Saumarez, put it like this:

... if at the end of our journey we find we are upon a wrong scent, our embarrassment will be great indeed.

When the fleet reached Alexandria, there wasn't a French ship in sight. Horatio ordered them to sail east along the Egyptian coast, but he knew that he was in big trouble. He was still only 39 and there were plenty of senior officers who had been angry at seeing a young upstart like him given command in the Mediterranean. They would be delighted if he made a mess of it. And at home, some of the people who had hailed Horatio as a hero the year before were starting to whinge.

THE SOLAR ORB

15th July 1798

NELSON: ALL WASHED UP?

Nautical nincompoop Nelson has lost the French fleet! The Orb says, come on, Admiral, pull your finger out! How can you lose 13 great big warships and nearly 400 frigates, troop-ships and supply craft? Have you tried looking down the back of the sofa? If you don't hurry up and find them, the French will soon be safe ashore and their ships snug in harbour!

Horatio's only consolation was that his captains still trusted him. Many of them were his own age or younger, and agreed with his ideas on how ships and battles should be run. Later he would look back happily on this long hunt around the Mediterranean, and call the captains who had served under him his 'band of brothers'.

After leaving Egypt, Horatio steered north up the coast of Palestine, then made for Crete. After that he headed for Sicily, afraid that the French might have landed there after all, but there was still no sign of them. Finally he turned towards Greece. At a small town called Koroni he sent Captain Troubridge ashore to question the governor.

Horatio went haring back to Alexandria. This time, the harbour was full of French ships, but they were only troop transports. Napoleon's army had gone ashore almost a month earlier, and had already gained control of the country.

As for the French warships, they were nowhere to be seen. It was all incredibly frustrating.

Horatio ordered the fleet to set sail again and sat down to a grumpy dinner. But just as he was about to tuck in…

But Horatio was not about to let the French escape again. Breuys had anchored his fleet in a line across the bay, with their guns pointing out to sea like floating fortresses. Horatio led his ships towards one end of the line, and sent two round into the shallow water behind the French so that they were attacking from both sides at once.

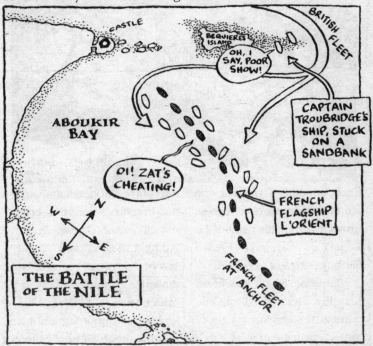

The French were caught off guard. They hadn't expected an attack from behind, and some of them hadn't even bothered opening their gun-ports on the landward side. Nor had they expected that the Brits would start a battle so late in the day. It was quarter past six in the evening when the first shots boomed out, marking the start of what would come to be known as the Battle of the Nile.

THE SOLAR ORB

5th September 1798

HIP HIP HORATIO

Kabbooooom! That was the sound that echoed across Aboukir Bay on the night of 1st August as the huge French flagship *L'Orient* exploded.

The blast, which was heard 15 miles away in Alexandria, came at the height of a fierce battle between No-good Nap's nasty navy and our own brave boys, commanded by Hot-shot Horatio Nelson, Britain's most huggable hero!

The battle had been raging for nearly three hours, with our brave sailors hammering the French, when fire broke out aboard *L'Orient*. French Admiral Brueys had already had both legs shot off and had made his men sit him up in a chair on the quarterdeck, where he kept giving orders until he was finally killed by a cannon ball. His helpless crew could do nothing to stop the flames spreading through their 120-gun, three-decker ship. Many jumped overboard in a desperate attempt to escape as flames licked at the masts and shone through the open gunports, fuelled by the stores of paint, oil and chemicals on the middle deck. At ten o'clock the fire reached the powder magazine and the huge ship was torn apart by a blast which flung broken planks, dead bodies, rigging, guns and fragments of hull high into the Egyptian night.

Brave Brueys: leg-less

For a few moments, gunners on the surrounding ships were too shocked to fire their pieces, and the silence was broken only by the splash of debris falling back into the sea, speckling the darkened bay with white flashes of foam.

Then the battle slowly started up again, and went on for almost eight more hours. By the end, some of our brave boys were so exhausted they fell asleep beside their guns. But VICTORY was ours, and although many of our ships were badly battered, none were sunk. Of the French, four were sunk and one burned, while seven more were captured. Only two, *Le Genereux* and Rear Admiral Villeneuve's flagship, the *Guillauime Tell* escaped. The victory leaves Napoleon's army stranded in Egypt. Somehow, we don't think he'll be giving us any more trouble!

As for man-of-the-match Horatio, he was wounded by a flying splinter early in the battle. It sliced his forehead open and covered him in blood, but he is up and about again and now plans to take his ship into Naples for repairs.

The ORB says: NICE ONE, NELSON!

NOBBLING NAPLES

It was September before news of the Battle of the Nile reached England. These days the whole thing would have been shown live on cable TV, but Horatio had to hand his report of the victory to a young officer, Captain Capel, who travelled back to London with it.

On the way, Capel stopped off at Naples to share the good news with Sir William and Lady Hamilton. When Emma heard it she was so excited that she fell down in a dead faint, but quickly recovered, bundled Capel and his friend Captain Hoste into her carriage and set off on a one-woman victory parade around the streets of Naples which lasted until long after dark.

She had a bandeau round her forehead with the words, 'Nelson and Victory'. The populace saw and understood what it meant, and 'Viva Nelson!' resounded through the streets!

Later, Emma sat down to write the conquering hero a letter. As you can see, her spelling and punctuation hadn't got any better.

Dearest Admiral Nelson
Tis impossible I can write for since Monday last I am delirious with joy and assure you I have a fever caused by agitation and pleasure. Good God, what a Victory! Never never has there been anything so glorious, anything half so complete ... I pity those who were not in the battle. I wou'd have rather been an English powder-monkey or a swab in that great battle than an emperor out of it ... I should feel it a glory to die in such a cause no I would not like to die till I see & embrace the Victor of the NILE ... How I glory in the Honner of my country and my countryman. I walk and tread in air with pride, feeling I was born in the same land with the victor Nelson and his gallant band ... My dress from head to foot is alla Nelson. Even my shawl is blue with gold anchors all over. My earrings are Nelson's anchors: in short we are be-Nelsoned all over.

Emma got even more excited a few weeks later, when battered Brit flagship the *Vanguard* limped into Naples for repairs, bringing battered Admiral Nelson with it. She wasn't put off by his missing arm or the nasty scars and bruises; she thought Horatio was fantastic. And she wasn't the only one. Naples had been living in fear of

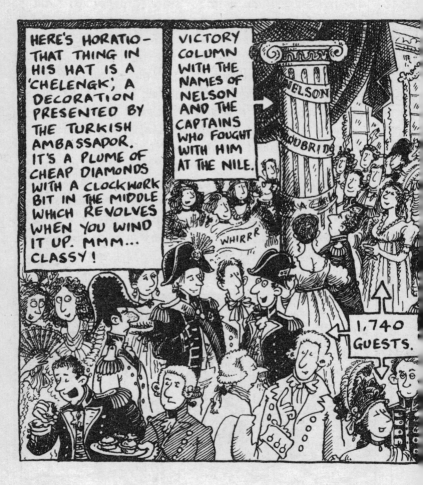

French invasion, ever since Napoleon's armies captured its northern neighbour, Rome. Nelson was the toast of the city. Sir William Hamilton invited him to come and stay at the Palazzo Sessa, and Emma set about preparing a spectacular ball to celebrate both the victory and Horatio's 40th birthday. It was a night to remember.

In England, celebrations of the victory were even more frantic. Captain Capel was mobbed by cheering crowds when he brought the news to London. Guns were fired, balls were organized, and illuminated transparencies appeared in the windows of shops and houses all over the country, showing pictures of Nelson and Britannia, and imaginary scenes of the great battle. A messenger was sent galloping down to Weymouth to deliver Horatio's report to the King, who was on holiday there. On the way, the messenger was stopped by a highwayman – but

when the highwayman learned what the man was carrying, he refused to hold him up and ordered him to ride on with all speed.

I MAY BE A RUTHLESS HIGHWAY ROBBER, BUT I'M A **BRITISH** RUTHLESS HIGHWAY ROBBER! HOORAY FOR NELSON!

Down in Norfolk, Fanny suddenly found that she was very popular with her fashionable neighbours – which annoyed her, as they had never wanted anything to do with her before. But what annoyed her more were Horatio's letters from Naples.

I hope one day to have the pleasure of introducing you to Lady Hamilton. She is one of the best women in the world...

She has a great soul...

She is an honour to her sex...

I'M SICK OF HEARING ABOUT LADY HAMILTON!

The trouble was, Emma and Horatio had fallen madly in love. It was inevitable really; they had so much in common. Emma thought Horatio was the most wonderful man in the whole world – and so did Horatio. She was always going on about how brave and glorious he was, which must have made a nice change from all those worried letters from Fanny pestering him to give up fighting and come and settle down in Norfolk. And when news came that the British Government was making Horatio a baron, Emma was furious. She thought he should be at least a viscount.

If I was King of England I would make you Duke Nelson, Marquis Nile, Earl Alexandria, Viscount Pyramid, Baron Crocodile and Prince Victory!

It wasn't long before all Naples was gossiping about Nelson and Lady Hamilton. What Emma's husband made of all this is hard to say. Sir William didn't seem to mind that his wife was spending nearly all her time with Horatio, and he always remained one of Horatio's friends. Perhaps he just thought it was inevitable that Emma would prefer a dashing naval hero to a dusty old vase collector, and decided to ignore it. Anyway, he was glad of Nelson's victory too...

Barmy armies and revolting Jacobins

For months before the Battle of the Nile, Sir William had been urging King Ferdinand to stop being neutral and join the Brits in their war with France. Now that Horatio had smashed the French fleet and Napoleon was stuck in Egypt, Ferdy started to think that might not be such a bad idea after all. Somebody dreamed up a cunning plan: King Ferdy's army should march north and recapture Rome from the French, with help from the Brits and Austrians. Ferdy wasn't sure, but Horatio and the Hamiltons were dead keen, and the Queen agreed with them. (Her sister Marie Antoinette had been beheaded by the French, remember, and she was eager for any chance to have a crack at them.)

The Neapolitan army wasn't up to much, so an old Austrian soldier called General Mack was sent to take command of the attack on Rome. (Though General Mack wasn't exactly a military genius either: he never travelled anywhere without a clumsy procession of five carriages to carry his staff, servants, spare outfits, toothbrush etc., and when he arranged some war games to show off his new army's skill, he lost.)

Horatio agreed that while General Mack and his army advanced on Rome from the south, he would land 4,000 infantry and 600 cavalry at Leghorn, to the north of the city, cutting off the French garrison. Meanwhile the

Austrians would attack the French armies in the north of Italy so that they couldn't send reinforcements.

At least, that was the plan. At the last minute, a message came from the Austrians.

Dear King F.
Sorry, can't make the war-please feel free to carry on without us.
Lots of love,
        the Austrians.

It was too late to cancel everything now. Ferdy had already announced his plans, so the French might launch a counterattack on Naples at any moment. Horatio told him he had a simple choice.

EITHER ADVANCE—OR STAY, AND BE KICKED OUT OF YOUR KINGDOM!

DOUBLE ☆*☺❀

As it turned out, Ferdy was going to advance *and* get kicked out of his kingdom.

At first everything went like clockwork. General Mack's army marched north, Horatio landed the troops at Leghorn and the French pulled out of Rome without firing a shot. King Ferdinand got to parade through the city with an escort of smartly uniformed dragoons and proclaim himself…

Horatio's work in Naples seemed to be done, and he decided it was time he nipped home to see Fanny and be adored a bit by the Brits before they forgot about his fabulous victory. But before he could leave there came worrying news from Rome.

THE NAPLES NEWS

18th December 1798

FRENCH SNATCH BACK ROME!

A French army has arrived outside Rome, and our brave boys are falling back towards Naples, heroically carrying all the loot they can manage. Our valiant King Ferdinand is at the very forefront of the retreat. When we asked him what he thought about these troubling developments he said, 'Get outta the way! Scarper! Women and kings first!!!'

It was soon clear that Ferdy's army had disintegrated, with most of its men running away at the first sight of a

Frenchman. Now the French were advancing on Naples, and there were rumours of a revolution brewing in the city. Unlike the French lower classes, the poor of Naples had always loved their king, and were still loyal to him – but the richer, better-educated types were sick to death of Ferdinand and Maria. A lot of them were Jacobins – supporters of the ideas of the French Revolution – and they planned to side with the French invaders and turn Naples into a republic.

Well, the poor weren't going to stand for that. They surrounded the royal palace, demanding that Ferdy organize a brave last stand against the French.

Ferdy had no intention of hanging around to face the fearsome French again. He arranged for Nelson to take him, the queen and their eight children to safety on the island of Sicily. The only problem was, how were they to get out of the palace without Ferdy's loyal subjects noticing that he was doing a bunk?

Luckily, the Turkish ambassador was giving a grand party on the evening of 21 December, and Horatio decided to delay the king's escape until then. He went to the party with the Hamiltons, telling their servants to pick them up later with their carriage ... but soon after dark they left the party on foot. Emma and Sir William decided it would be wisest to leave with their friends, the king and queen. They hurried down to the harbour and went aboard the *Vanguard*. Meanwhile, Horatio went to the palace and snuck the royal family out through a secret passage without any of their people noticing.

Unfortunately the weather was too bad for the *Vanguard* to sail that night, and she had to stay at anchor in the bay of Naples for several more days. The Neapolitans soon realized that their royals were deserting them, and sent boats out to beg Ferdy to stay and help them fight the French – but all Ferdy cared about was getting away as fast as possible.

At last, on 23 December the *Vanguard* was able to set sail. But early the following morning she ran into the worst storm Horatio had ever known.

THE QUEEN'S YOUNGEST CHILD, PRINCE CARLO ALBERTO, WENT INTO CONVULSIONS.

SIR WILLIAM HID IN HIS CABIN WITH TWO LOADED PISTOLS.

I'M NOT GOING TO DROWN! AS SOON AS THE SHIP STARTS TO SINK, I'LL SHOOT MYSELF!

With the sailors busy fighting to keep the ship afloat, it was up to Emma to look after the other passengers. She gave the royal family all her bedclothes (they had forgotten to bring their own), and helped mop up the sick, as well as doing her best to comfort the frightened children … but sadly there was nothing to do for poor Prince Carlo, who was so weakened by seasickness that he died in her arms early on Christmas Day.

On Boxing Day the bruised and battered *Vanguard* finally dropped anchor at Palermo (the main city of Sicily and King Ferdy's southern capital). The cowardly king was delighted to be safely out of Naples and immediately got ready to go on a hunting trip in one of his royal parks, but Maria was grief-stricken over Prince Carlo's death. Sir William was grief-stricken too, but not over the poor little Prince; he had just heard that the ship which had been taking his vase collection back to England had sunk. He fell ill and took to his bed, leaving

Emma and Horatio free to carry on their love affair even more openly than before.

But in spite of Emma's company, Horatio was sick and miserable in Sicily, and depressed over the failure of the attack on Rome – another disaster which was partly his fault.

He was even more depressed when he heard the latest news from Naples…

THE PARTHENOPEAN NEWS

(Formerly The Naples News)   23rd January 1799

NAPLES WELCOMES THE FRENCH

A French army entered Naples today, quickly overpowering the royalist garrison and stamping out any resistance from the angry citizens. The Jacobins have made them welcome, and announced that from now on Naples will be known as the Parthenopean Republic, after the ancient Greek city of Parthenope which once stood here.

A spokesman for the new republic said today, "We can't thank the French enough for getting rid of King Big-nose for us. We're sick of being ruled by a corrupt royal family and their allies the Catholic Church. We want to be modern and forward thinking, like they are in France."

FREE! REVOLUTIONARY HAT! AS WORN IN FRANCE! SEE PAGE 346.

The new government set to work at once, getting rid of all signs of the monarchy and dragging their city kicking and screaming into the nineteenth century.

- They started calling each other 'Citizen', just like the French revolutionaries.
- They wore nice floppy red caps, just like the French revolutionaries.

- They staged improving puppet shows to teach people about republicanism.
- They gave streets named after kings and saints new, republican names.

- They erected a Tree of Liberty (a sort of republican Christmas tree with a floppy red cap on) in every public square.
- They suggested that anybody called Ferdinand should find himself a new name.

The Parthenopeans weren't a bad bunch as revolutionaries go – staging puppet shows and changing street names is better than chopping peoples' heads off, after all. They wanted to make Naples a more free and equal place. There was just one problem:

129

Meanwhile, King Ferdy was perfectly happy in Palermo, slaughtering the local wildlife. But Queen Maria wasn't about to let the Jacobins get away with booting her out of Naples and killing her little boy. She started nagging Ferdy to organize a counterattack. Her friend Emma Hamilton nagged him too, until Ferdy was so sick of her that he said he felt like throwing her out of the nearest window.

Another person keen to recapture Naples was one of the King's advisors, a priest called Cardinal Ruffo who had a fanatical hatred of all Jacobins. He offered to go to Calabria (the area south of Naples) and gather an army to crush the new republic.

Soon Ruffo was storming towards Naples at the head of a rough old mob of about 20,000 Calabrian peasants and brigands.

Horatio had been in a foul mood ever since he arrived in Sicily, and he didn't trust Ruffo, but he still agreed to lend his ships to help in the attack. They went on ahead of him, commanded by Captain Troubridge, and captured the islands off the coast of Naples. By summer the Army of the Holy Faith had stormed into the city itself ... and they weren't behaving in a very Christian way.

WE LOOTED ANY HOUSES WITH RICH FURNISHINGS – WELL, THEY MUST BELONG TO JACOBINS, MUSTN'T THEY? AND WE SHOT LOADS OF REBELS AND THEIR FAMILIES AND CUT THEIR HEADS OFF AND STUCK THEM ON POLES.

THEY MAKE GREAT FOOTBALLS, TOO!

BOOT

Eventually even Cardinal Ruffo started to fear that his army was out of control. Eager to end the fighting, he made a deal with the French, who still controlled some of the city's strongholds. If they surrendered...
• they would be shipped home to France.
• Neapolitans who had supported the Parthenopean Republic would be pardoned and allowed to return to their homes.
The French agreed, but their Neapolitan friends still thought they would be better off out of the city when King Ferdy returned, so they decided to sail for France as well. The only thing stopping them was Horatio.

Nelson gets nasty

Horatio arrived back in Naples soon after Cardinal Ruffo did his deal, bringing Emma and Sir William with him (Ferdy and Maria were staying safely in Palermo until all the trouble was over, of course). As far as he was concerned, the Neapolitan Jacobins were the lowest form of life. After all, they had turned against their king, and Horatio still had a bit of a thing about kings, even foreign ones. He was furious when he heard what terms Cardinal Ruffo had agreed to.

YOU ARRANGED THIS TRUCE WITHOUT THE KING'S PERMISSION! THE FRENCH MUST SURRENDER WITHOUT CONDITIONS! AND THE NEAPOLITAN REBELS MUST ALL STAND TRIAL AS TRAITORS!

BUT I'VE GIVEN THEM MY WORD! THE BOATS ARE WAITING TO TAKE THEM TO FRANCE!

Horatio decided to ignore the truce that the Cardinal had arranged, and what happened next was one of the strangest and nastiest parts of his story.

First, he sent a message to King Ferdy back in Palermo, asking him to decide what should be done. Meanwhile, with violence and chaos still raging in Naples, he agreed that the defeated rebels should be allowed to go aboard the small merchant ships (called 'polaccas') which were waiting to take them to safety. But they were not allowed to leave the harbour.

Soon afterwards, Queen Maria sent word from Palermo, completely agreeing with Horatio.

AN EXAMPLE MUST BE MADE OF THE REBELS! THE WOMEN WHO TOOK PART MUST BE TREATED JUST LIKE THE MEN— WITHOUT PITY!

The refugees' polaccas were immediately brought alongside the waiting British warships and put under an armed guard, while Ruffo's men prepared to start trying them for treason. (Many of the refugees thought that they had only been allowed to board at all so that Nelson could get them all under his control.) One of the people on the polaccas turned out to be Prince Carraciolo, the former commander of King Ferdy's fleet. When the rebels took charge of Naples they had forced him to stay on as admiral, or face a firing squad – but Horatio didn't think that was any excuse; to him, Carraciolo was no better than a mutineer, and there was only one punishment for mutiny...

HANG HIM FROM THE YARDARM OF THE SICILIAN FLAGSHIP! THEN THROW HIS BODY INTO THE SEA!

Two days after the admiral's hanging, King Ferdy came back to Naples – but he still didn't trust his people enough to actually go ashore. He set up his court aboard Horatio's flagship in the bay and lived there for the next few weeks, holding sumptuous dinner parties and receiving visitors on the quarterdeck. In the evenings, Emma Hamilton would play her harp and musicians would come alongside in boats to serenade the royal party. The only thing that spoiled the jolly holiday mood was Prince Carriacolo's corpse, which popped up from the bottom of the sea one day to join the fun, in spite of having been weighted down with 250 lbs of lead. Here's what Midshipman George Parsons saw when he went on deck that morning…

I … found His Majesty gazing with intense anxiety on some distant object. At once he turned pale and, letting his spyglass fall on deck, uttered an exclamation of horror. My eyes instinctively turned in the same direction and, under our larboard quarter, with his face full upon us, much swollen and discoloured by the water, and his [eyes] started from their sockets by strangulation, floated the ill-fated prince.

Ferdy was so afraid that a priest was called, who calmed him down by telling him that Carriacolo had only come back to ask the king's forgiveness, and should be towed ashore and given a Christian burial. So that was all right then.

> *The unlooked for appearance of Carraciolo's corpse did not lessen our appetite for the good things in the king's larder, or our zest for the evening's opera.*

Meanwhile, boatload after boatload of rebels from the polaccas were being taken ashore to stand trial. Men and women alike were tortured in the prisons before being dragged to a public square and hanged in front of a jeering crowd, while the hangman swung on their legs and a dwarf capered about on their shoulders. The executions went on and on for months, and by the time the polaccas were finally allowed to sail for France almost two-thirds of the rebels who had gone aboard them had been executed.

> *We are restoring happiness to the kingdom of Naples, and doing justice to millions.*

King Ferdinand was so grateful for Horatio's help that he arranged a huge victory celebration for him back in Palermo, and gave him a diamond-studded sword and the Dukedom of Bronte. (Bronte was a town on the slopes of Mount Etna, the volcano where the one-eyed giants of Greek and Roman legend were supposed to have lived – so maybe Ferdy was having a little joke at the one-eyed admiral's expense.)

Horatio was over the moon about his new title. The farms and tenants on his new land would add about another £3,000 a year to his piggy bank, and he even got a shiny new decoration to wear on his coat, next to the star of the Order of the Bath. From then on he would always sign his name:

Nelson Bronte

FURIOUS FANNY
AND LITTLE HORATIA

While Horatio was parading around Palermo covered with medals and dukedoms and diamond-studded swords, the Admiralty was starting to get a bit cheesed off. After all, Lord Nelson was supposed to be working for them, not some big-nosed foreign king. He had been so busy pasting the poor Parthenopean Republic that he had twice refused the Admiralty's orders to send some of his ships to help defend Minorca, which was being threatened by the French. (If anyone else had done that, Horatio might have called it mutiny, but of course he didn't think such rules applied to him.)

Then, at the end of August, came some worrying news...

NOW I SHALL 'AVE MYSELF DECLARED FIRST CONSUL! (ZAT MEANS RULER OF FRANCE, IN CASE YOU ARE TOO THEEK TO WERK IT OUT.)

It looked as though the war wasn't over by a long chalk, and people were starting to say that Horatio's fling with Emma Hamilton was interfering with his work.

She leads him about like a keeper with a bear!

He is completely managed by Lady Hamilton!

Their gambling is talked of everywhere!

There were some unlikely stories being told, as well.

SIR WILLIAM HAS CHALLENGED NELSON TO A DUEL!

LADY H. AND THE ADMIRAL VISIT THE WATERFRONT TAVERNS, DISGUISED AS A COMMON SAILOR AND HIS GIRL!

Lord Keith, the new commander-in-chief of the Brit's Mediterranean fleet, wasn't impressed when he visited Horatio in Palermo at the start of 1800…

THEY'RE A PAIR OF SILLY, LOVE-STRUCK TWITS!

When Lord Keith left Palermo he made sure Horatio went with him. They sailed towards Malta, which had been occupied by the French, and on the way there Horatio fought and captured the *Genereux*, one of the ships which had got away at the Battle of the Nile, which cheered him up no end. Maybe he did secretly realize how badly he had been behaving, because he seemed relieved to be back at sea again, and Lord Keith left him in charge of the blockade of Malta. But after a few days, Horatio turned round and sailed back to Emma in Palermo, complaining that he didn't feel well.

Soon afterwards he got a snappy letter from the First Lord of the Navy, ordering him to return to England.

Horatio wasn't sure that he wanted to go home. He must have known the stories about him and Emma which were going around back in London, and he can't have looked forward to having to explain things to Fanny. But the Hamiltons were going home too; Sir William's health was failing and he was being replaced by another ambassador. Horatio decided that they could all travel together.

OH, HOW NICE.

Horatio had been hoping that he and the Hamiltons would all sail home in style aboard his flagship, but Lord Keith put his foot down. With Napoleon back in charge the French were on the move again, and he wanted to keep all the ships he could in the Mediterranean. Besides...

> Lady Hamilton has had command of the fleet long enough...

...so Horatio and his friends ended up travelling back by land, stopping on the way at Vienna, Prague, Dresden and a lot of small German cities. Wherever they went there were celebrations to welcome the hero of the Nile. As the only man in Europe who had outwitted the great Napoleon, he was treated like a cross between a famous popstar and the man who's just scored the winning goal in the World Cup Final. Balls, concerts and firework displays were held in his honour, and people travelled from all over Europe to meet him. One old German pastor came 40 miles to ask Horatio to sign the Bible from his village church.

But not everybody was so impressed…

…*a more miserable collection of skin and bones and wizened frame I have yet to come across. He was almost covered with ribbons and stars.*

He seemed as clumsy and dim on land as he is adroit and notable at sea.

…and as for Emma…

She is bold, forward, coarse, assuming and vain!

She's the fattest woman I've ever set eyes on!

She drinks an extraordinary amount of champagne!

What none of them seemed to have noticed was that Emma was already six months pregnant with Horatio's child.

Home sweet home

At last, on 6th November 1800, Horatio and the others reached England. There were cheering crowds to welcome him when he landed at Great Yarmouth, and he stood on the balcony of an inn to wave to them, accompanied by Emma, who was wearing a gown embroidered with the words, 'Nelson' and 'Bronte'. Later, the inn's landlady had a favour to ask, and Horatio had the chance to make a hilarious joke...

Well, maybe it was the way he said it.

In London, crowds were waiting to cheer him, even though it was pouring with rain. But Fanny did not give him such a warm welcome. She had been upset by the stories she had heard, and her first meeting with Emma and Sir William was probably one of the most embarrassing dinner parties in history.

Edmund Nelson was horrified by Horatio's behaviour too, and sided with Fanny. So did much of London high society. When Horatio continued being seen with Emma at theatres and balls it was taken as an insult to his poor wife. It wasn't long before Horatio started turning from a national hero into a national joke.

THE SOLAR ORB

18th December 1800

COLD SHOULDER FOR LOVE-RAT NELSON!

Horatio Nelson may be the toast of London's merchants and common people, but he's not popular with the nobs!

At St James Palace he arrived to meet the King dressed up like a Christmas tree, covered in medals and ribbons and wearing a clockwork plume of diamonds in his hat! Not surprisingly, good King George gave him a frosty welcome!

And he's not the only one. Nifty Nelson may have nobbled Nap at the Nile, but the *Orb* can exclusively reveal that he's not welcome at any of the posh parties this season. 'He's treating poor dear Lady Nelson in the most abominable manner,' said one society hostess. 'He won't be welcome at my house, and all my friends feel the same way!'

The *Orb* has learned that the naughty admiral won't even be staying in London for Christmas. Instead, he and the Hamiltons will be lying low at Fonthill Abbey, country home of potty moneybags William Beckford. Needless to say, Lady Nelson hasn't been invited!

It was when Horatio returned from Fonthill after Christmas that things finally came to a head.

that she can live on for at least a year at my house in London. I never mean to see her again.

Honestly, she's been so unreasonable! Why can't she see that Emma and I are meant to be together? She should have behaved with a bit more understanding, like Sir William. At least he doesn't kick up a fuss when Em and I want to spend time together... (Although I do sometimes wish he would hurry up and die — then I would have Em to myself!)

Poor Emma! Her child is due soon. I wish I could be with her, but I fear it wouldn't do. The London newspapers do not understand our situation any better than Fanny, and have begun printing horrid slanders about us - vulgar verses, and foolish cartoons. They say that Em is 'huge', and the silly artists draw her as big as an elephant! Emma isn't fat! She's just well-rounded. Idiots!

Thank Heaven I can escape to sea. I have been appointed second in command of the Channel Fleet and shall go aboard my new flagship at once. While I am away Emma and I will write to each other in code, in case anyone finds our letters and makes them public. I am going to pretend that one of my sailors, Thompson, is in love with one of Emma's servants, who is about to have a baby. Of course, there isn't really a Thompson, nor any servant— it's just a way for Em to let me know how she is!

Cunning, eh?

HN ❤ EH

22nd January

Aboard my new flagship the San Josef, one of the ships we captured at the Battle of the Nile (thanks to ME) and part of the Channel Fleet, which protects our shores from the wicked French. Unfortunately I am second in command to Lord

St Vincent, which is a bit embarrassing, as I'm in the middle of a lawsuit against him. The old scoundrel claims that £20,000 of my prize money from my victories in the Med should go to him, since he was officially in command of the fleet there at the time! Pah! I didn't notice _him_ helping at ~~half~~ Naples. Honour and glory are all very well, but I can't afford to let that sort of money slip through my fingers...

Missing E very much, and wish I had not left her in London.

28th January 1801

MY CABIN

lonely sigh

Atrocious news! While I am away, Sir William has had the Prince of Wales to dine at his house! Everyone knows the Prince has an eye for the ladies! I am sure he is trying to steal Emma from me! It's a disgrace! What is Sir William

thinking of! Doesn't he care what happens to E's reputation? I have written her a sharp letter, warning her not to flirt with the P of W...

5th February 1801

Wonderful news! E's child is born! We have a little girl!

Horatio was as pleased as punch to think that he was a daddy at last – but there was no way he could share the good news with anybody else. Having babies with people you weren't married to was a terribly scandalous thing to do in those days, and if word got round about the little girl it would mean disgrace for Horatio and Emma – and for the child, when she grew up. So nobody knew that Emma had had a baby, except for her servants (who didn't count), her doctor (who wasn't letting on), and Sir William (who politely pretended not to have noticed).

All Horatio could do was write letter after letter to Emma (four a day sometimes), and dream up mad schemes for the christening...

Dearest darling Emma, darling.

I think the christening should take place at the Church of St George in Hanover Square, where you and Sir W were married. Of course we cannot let on that we are the sweet child's mother and father, but we could claim that she is an orphan and that we have agreed to pay for her christening and upbringing. We could call her Emma, which is the prettiest name in the world. And I have a particularly cunning idea: we shall say her parents were JOHEM and MORATA ETNORB. If you read ETNORB backwards and mix up the letters of the other two names and change the J for an I you'll see just how cunning it is!

Lots of love and kisses from
    your ever-loving

        ♡ Horatio

Luckily, Emma still had her head screwed on.

Dear darling Horatio oops I meen Admiral Nelson, darling, dear.

Thankyou for your last letter, but do you not think the vicar might be a bit surprized if he had to do a christening for Johem and Morata Etnorb? And people might gossip if we was to be there - espeshially if you change your will to mention the baby — you know what nasty suspishus minds they've got.

Please do not do anything just yet. I have sent ~~out~~ I meen Mr Thompson's little treasure to live with a woman called Mrs Gibson. Nobody noticed me take her there; I hid her under my muff. Mrs Gibson has been paid and will bring up the baby with her own daughter. So no-one will ever know she is the child of the mighty ~~NELSON~~ sorry I meen Mr Thompson.

Heaps of love and cuddles from ♡
Emma × × × × × × × × ♡

PS: Sorry, we can't call her Emma that's what I called my last baby, who might still be alive for all I know. Let's call her HORATIA.

Righto, Napoleon. Let's leave Nelson skipping about for joy and take a quick look at whatever it is you've been up to since you got back from Egypt.

Tsar wars

Meanwhile, Tsar Paul, ruler of Russia, was behaving a bit strangely. Russia had been against France all through the war. Now potty Paul decided to switch sides. He didn't actually declare war on the Brits, but he set about persuading his neighbours to form a sort of anti-British club.

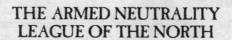

THE ARMED NEUTRALITY LEAGUE OF THE NORTH

MEMBERS: Russia, Prussia, Denmark, Sweden and Norway*

*Norway are ruled by Sweden anyway so they're in whether they like it or not.

RULES:

1. No more trade with Britain.
2. No more war with France – we'll trade with them instead.
3. Everybody has to say how brilliant I am.
4. Er...

The Armed Neutrality was bad news for the Brits. If they couldn't trade with the northern powers they wouldn't be able to get hold of the timber, tar, canvas, hemp, copper and iron that they needed to build warships and keep them afloat. They decided to send a large fleet north to persuade Russia's neighbours not to join. First in command would be doddery old Admiral Sir Hyde Parker. Second in command would be...

Meanwhile, Horatio had been in London, getting to know his new daughter.

A finer child was never produced by two persons.

BURP!
DRIBBLE!

POO!

But he didn't have long to enjoy being a daddy, because after only a few days he was ordered to sea again, bound for the Danish capital Copenhagen.

DUFFING UP THE DANES

As usual, it took ages for the fleet to get organized. This was partly because British diplomats were still looking for an easier way to stop Tsar Paul forming his club, and partly because Admiral Parker was a bit of an old skiver. He and Horatio didn't hit it off at all.

Secret Log Book of H. Nelson

6th March 1801

This is ridiculous! I arrived at Yarmouth in my new flagship the St George today and found our fleet still hanging about, stores not yet loaded and old Sir Hyde Parker staying at a comfy inn on shore. It seems he has found himself a new wife, and he would rather be snuggled up with her than out here in the cold wind doing his duty. (I hear she's a fat little thing. Our sailors

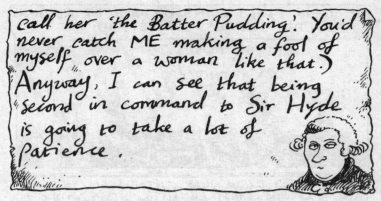

call her 'the Batter Pudding'. You'd never catch ME making a fool of myself over a woman like that.) Anyway, I can see that being second in command to Sir Hyde is going to take a lot of patience.

The Admiralty was losing patience with Sir Hyde as well. After a week of his dithering they sent word that he was to sail AT ONCE. Sir Hyde hadn't even got round to giving out his orders to the captains under his command, so you can imagine the chaos at Yarmouth when he suddenly told them to be ready to sail at midnight.

At last they left for Denmark. But Sir Hyde still wasn't sure what they were going to do when they got there. He invited Horatio and a British Diplomat called Vansittart aboard his flagship to talk it over.

I SAY WE BLOCKADE THE LEAGUE'S PORTS, THEN SIT BACK AND WAIT. MAYBE THEY'LL JUST GET BORED AND GIVE UP.

BUT I'VE JUST GOT BACK FROM DENMARK! THEY'RE PREPARING FOR WAR!

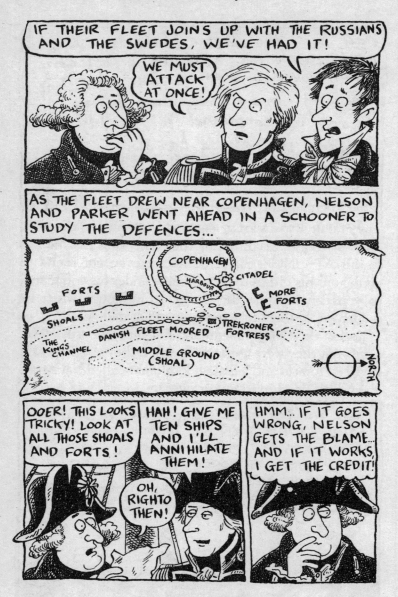

The Battle of Copenhagen

Secret Log Book of H. Nelson

2nd April 1801

Well, I don't like to sound bigheaded, but I really am the most astounding naval genius in the entire history of the world ever!

Sir Hyde gave me command of 12 sail-of-the-line, and 27 smaller ships. This morning we began our attack on the Danish fleet. It was like the Nile all over again, with the Danes at anchor in a long line. They must have thought they were pretty safe, what with that great shoal between them and us, and protected by the guns of their forts.

It looked dicey at first, I must admit. Three of my ships ran aground as we sailed into the King's Channel, and the forts opened up with a thunderous bombardment and clouds of smoke filling the air with shot and splinters.

MIDDLE GROUND

SHIPS AGROUND

157

That fool Parker who was watching from his flagship, safely out of range, thought we were taking a beating and panicked. He hoisted signal flags ordering me to break off the battle! "

" Of course I wasn't going to obey! I told my officers, 'I only have one eye. I have a right to be blind sometimes.' Then I put the telescope to my blind eye and said 'I really do not see the signal.'

Rather clever, I thought... Must remember to tell Emma. "

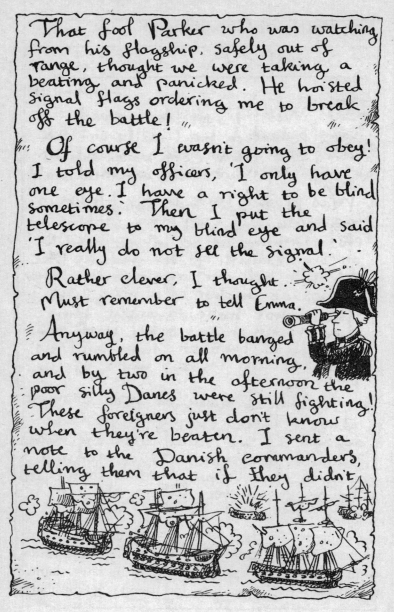

" Anyway, the battle banged and rumbled on all morning, and by two in the afternoon the poor silly Danes were still fighting! These foreigners just don't know when they're beaten. I sent a note to the Danish commanders, telling them that if they didn't cease firing at once I would burn all the ships I'd captured. A Danish officer came out and arranged a truce, and so the battle ended. Another famous victory — though sad to say we lost 1,000 sailors and three captains and six of my ships are now aground.

Was rowed back to Sir Hyde's flagship, half expecting to be court-martialled for disobeying orders. Instead he seemed to be very pleased with me. Funny chap.

Then to bed. Very tired, but shall write to my guardian angel E before I sleep and let her know the good news.

The day after the battle Nelson was rowed ashore to meet the Danish Crown Prince. The Danes provided a carriage to take him to their Amalienborg Palace, but Horatio preferred to walk, and the people of Copenhagen lined the streets to watch him pass. Although he had spent the whole of the previous day bombarding their ships and fortresses he later claimed that the Danes cheered him. His friend Captain Hardy, who went with him, said: 'Lord Nelson was met with as much acclamation as when we went to the Lord Mayor's Show!' A Danish eyewitness said the people were polite but silent – but at least they didn't boo: 'They did not degrade themselves with cheers, nor disgrace themselves with murmurs.'

Negotiations between Horatio and the Danish government continued on and off for almost a week. It was a strange situation, for although the two countries had just fought a terrible battle, they weren't actually at war. But Horatio's message to the Danish Crown Prince was quite simple.

Eventually the Danes agreed (though only to a 14-week truce, not 16) and Horatio went back to the waiting fleet. Sir Hyde Parker now sailed on to deal with Sweden and Russia. Nelson was left behind when the wind dropped, leaving his ship becalmed, but he was so determined not to miss a good fight that he made some of his sailors row him through the night in an open boat to catch up with the others. Unfortunately he forgot to take his cloak with him, and by the time he reached Parker he had caught a nasty chill.

Meanwhile, Parker had already sent a message into the Swedish port of Karlskrona.

Dear Swedish sorts,
You've probably heard about that 14-week cease-fire the Danes have just signed up to? It really would be awfully nice if you'd do the same.
Thanks everso!
Sir Hyde Parker.

The Swedes replied.

THEY SAY THEY'LL THINK IT OVER, SIR HYDE.

BUT WE CAN'T SAIL ON TO RUSSIA IF THEY WON'T SIGN! THEY MIGHT ATTACK US FROM BEHIND! QUICK, BACK TO DENMARK!

What with one thing and another, Sir Hyde wasn't making a very good impression on his bosses at the Admiralty, and when he reached Copenhagen again he got a letter from them ordering him to hand over command of the fleet to Nelson and return home. There was talk among the sailors that he would face a court martial for his timid behaviour when he got there, but Horatio hoped not: 'His friends in the fleet wish everything to be forgot, for we all respect and love Sir Hyde; but the dearer his friends, the more uneasy they have been at his idleness.'

Now there was no anxious admiral to hold him back, Horatio sailed straight to the Russian naval base at Reval. But while he had been busy clobbering Copenhagen there had been big changes in Russia. Tsar Paul had been assassinated by his own bodyguards (who brained him with a paperweight), and the new Tsar, his son Alexander, wasn't so keen on cosying up to Napoleon, and soon disbanded the Armed Neutrality League.

THE FRENCH ARE COMING!
(MAYBE...)

Horatio came home from the Baltic in the summer of 1801, but not to the sort of hero's welcome he thought he deserved.

HELLO! I'M BACK!

The British people hated the French, but they had never really had anything against the Danes...

I HAVE!

...well, not for about 800 years, anyway. The Battle of Copenhagen didn't seem like something to celebrate, and even if it had, they probably wouldn't have been in the mood; they had something else to worry about...

THE SOLAR ORB

15th July 1801

(C)RAFTY FROGS BARGE IN!

Fears are growing that Beastly Bonaparte and his Foul French are planning to INVADE our wonderful country!

A French invasion would mean:

- British freedom crushed by a foreign dictator!
- Our Protestant Church of England replaced by the Catholic Church!
- Funny-shaped bread!

Nasty Nap is massing thousands of soldiers and landing barges in the harbours of northern France. They are just waiting for a calm night so that they can row across the channel and attack England!

There are also rumours that Nap's engineers are planning to dig a tunnel beneath the channel, and construct giant windmill-powered invasion rafts, just like the one in this convincing artist's impression!

The ORB says: Government must ACT NOW to save us from disaster!

The Admiralty wasn't convinced that a French invasion could succeed. As Lord St Vincent said: 'I do not say that the French cannot come. I only say that they cannot come by sea.' But preparations had to be made just in case, if only to calm the public's nerves.

And what better way to calm them than by appointing everybody's fave admiral to head the defence forces?

After coming home from Copenhagen, Horatio had gone off on holiday to Surrey with Emma, Sir William and one of Horatio's officers, a young captain named Edward Parker. (Poor Horatia was left in London with Mrs Gibson.) He was recalled to duty at once, and given command of a squadron of frigates, brigs and floating gun-batteries which were supposed to smash the French invasion barges if they tried to cross the Channel. He was also in charge of the Sea Fencibles, a volunteer force of fishermen and boat-owners from the coastal towns who were to help the Navy if the French attacked.

Horatio wasn't altogether happy in his new job. It was mostly paperwork and organization, and since he was supposed to stay aboard his ship, anchored off Dover, he had no chance of seeing Emma.

<u>The *Secret Log Book* of H. Nelson</u>

20th July 1801.

I am convinced that the Admiralty is deliberately stopping me from seeing Em. They say it reassures the public to know that I am always at my post, so here I must stay. It is all Troubridge's doing! He used to be my friend – he owes his new job at the Admiralty to me – but he has taken Fanny's side and will do

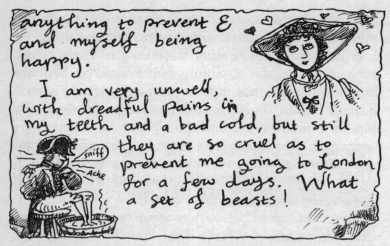

anything to prevent E
and myself being
happy.

I am very unwell,
with dreadful pains in
my teeth and a bad cold, but still
they are so cruel as to
prevent me going to London
for a few days. What
a set of beasts!

It wasn't only loneliness and toothache that got Horatio down that summer. He hated hanging about at anchor, waiting for the French. So, when he wasn't busy scribbling love letters to Emma, he set about planning a few surprises for them. On 1 August he took a small squadron to look into Boulogne harbour and let off a few shots at the ships moored there. A couple of days later, crowds watched from the cliffs at Dover while some of his ships fought a running battle with a small French force out in the Channel. But these skirmishes were just a beginning: Nelson was working up to something much more ambitious.

He decided to launch a night attack on Boulogne. It was to be a 'cutting out' expedition, with men sneaking up in small boats to slice through the mooring ropes of French ships, which could then be brought back to England as prizes. The attack force was to consist of four groups of flat-bottomed boats carrying sailors armed with pikes, cutlasses, muskets, bayonets and tomahawks. One of the groups was to be led by Horatio's young friend Edward Parker, but Horatio himself did not take part; he had promised Emma that he would not lead this attack in person. If he had, things might have turned out differently. As it was, just like the attack on Tenerife back in 1798, the expedition to Boulogne turned into a total dog's dinner.

Forty five British sailors died that night, and 130 were wounded, including Parker, whose leg was shattered by a musket ball.

Horatio, who was probably feeling guilty now for not planning the attack better and leading it in person, took lodgings for Edward Parker in Deal, where he visited him constantly and did everything he could to help him recover.

I would lose a dozen limbs to serve him, my friend, my nurse, my attendant, my protector.

Sadly, the wounded leg turned bad and had to be sawn off, and soon afterwards Parker died.

Horatio was heartbroken. He cried openly at Parker's funeral, and claimed that he was 'grieved almost to death'. To make matters worse, other sea officers were grumbling about the botched battle at Boulogne. Horatio longed to mount another attack and make amends for his failure, but he wasn't sure where or how to strike.

But at least there was one bit of good news to take his mind off it all. Earlier in the year he had started looking for a new house where he could live with Emma, and now she wrote to say that she had found the ideal place...

THE GREAT MERTON MAKEOVER

Fibb, Floggit & Scram
Estate Agents to the Rich & Gullible

FOR SALE

MERTON PLACE

A delightful two-storey country house. Handy for London. Would suit a gentleman and his family. Established garden complete with ornamental canal. Needs some small alterations. A snip at only £9000.

Nine thousand pounds might not sound like a lot of money for a country house, but in 1801 it was a fair bit – the equivalent of £550,000 today. Buying Merton ate up almost all Horatio's savings. And those small alterations wouldn't come cheap, either.

WE'LL NEED SOME MORE WINDOWS, AND SOME VERANDAS, AND AN UNDERPASS TO LINK THE HOUSE TO THE OUTBUILDINGS ON THE FAR SIDE OF THE ROAD, AND ALL THE ROOMS ON THE GROUND FLOOR NEED ENLARGING. OOH, AND I FANCY A COUPLE OF THOSE NEW-FANGLED INDOOR LOOS!

Horatio couldn't even rely on future victories and prize money to help him pay for it all, because the invasion scare had come to nothing and the war with France was finally winding down.

THE SOLAR ORB

1st October 1801

PEACE BREAKS OUT!

A peace treaty was signed today in the French town of Amiens, bringing to an end nine long years of war.

There was rejoicing in the streets of London when the good news was announced, and when the French ambassador made his way to meet King George his carriage was dragged along by cheering crowds.

Horatio wasn't at all sure that peace was a good idea, and not just because it would mean he was out of a job. The truth was that France got far more out of the Treaty of Amiens than Britain, which had to give up a lot of valuable naval bases in places like Minorca and the

Cape of Good Hope as part of the agreement. Besides, he still didn't trust the French.

Still, the end of the war meant that the Admiralty had no more excuse for keeping Horatio stuck aboard his ship at Dover. As soon as he could get ashore he rushed up to Merton to see his new house for the first time and to be reunited with Emma, who had already moved in. Horatio was delighted, and called his dream house 'Paradise Merton'. The only fly in the ointment was the fact that Sir William Hamilton was living there as well as Emma.

MERTON PLACE

ORNAMENTAL CANAL, NICKNAMED 'THE NILE' BY EMMA AND HORATIO.

SIR WILLIAM ENJOYS A SPOT OF FISHING.

Sir William was resigned to Emma and Horatio's affair by now, and kept himself to himself. Also, although Sir William paid a third of the running costs for Merton, Horatio refused to let him clutter the place up with any of his old vases, which had to stay at the Hamiltons' London home. Instead, the new house became a sort of museum to Horatio and Emma. One visitor, Lord Minto, described it like this:

> *Not only the rooms but the whole house, staircase and all, are covered with nothing but pictures of her and him ... and representations of his naval actions, coats of arms, pieces of plate in his honour, the flagstaff of L'Orient etc. If it was Lady Hamilton's house there might be a pretence for this, but to make his own a mere looking glass to view himself all day is bad taste.*

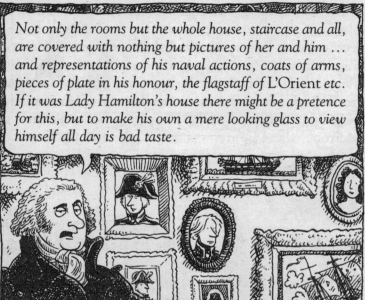

Horatio didn't see much of his posh new neighbours, most of whom didn't approve of him and Emma living together, but he had plenty of visits from friends and relatives to keep him occupied – although Horatia was still hidden away in London. One of the visitors was Horatio's father – although it took a lot of persuading to get him to stay at Merton. Edmund Nelson was very fond of Fanny, and had been terribly distressed by the way his son had dumped her. Now, old and frail, he was thinking of going to live with her at her house in London. Not surprisingly, Horatio didn't think much of that idea.

Nor did Emma. She loathed Fanny, and thought that she was just trying to stir up trouble with her kindness to Edmund.

> His poor father is taken in by a very wicked woman acting a bad part!

In the end, Edmund didn't go to live with Fanny, and he did accept Horatio's invitation to spend some time at Merton (where Emma was very kind to him). It was to be the last time Horatio saw his father. Edmund spent that winter in Bath as usual, and the following spring, word came that he was dying. Fanny rushed from London to be with him, but Horatio wouldn't go; he was scared of the embarrassment if he bumped into his wife. He didn't attend the funeral for the same reason. But he did grieve for the old man, and insisted that everyone at Merton Place join him in mourning. His niece Charlotte, who was staying there at the time, said: '... my uncle is very particular that all possible respect should be paid to my grandpapa's memory. He would not let (my brother) go a-fishing ... nor do we see anybody. My spirits are worn out seeing my uncle's suffering.'

Horatio in the house

Now that the war was over, Horatio needed something else to do, and he decided to try his hand at politics. He had been made a viscount after the victory at Copenhagen, which meant that he was entitled to sit in the House of Lords.

AND I GET THIS SNAZZY ERMINE ROBE!

Unfortunately, he wasn't much use as a politician. One of his first speeches was a defence of some of the terms of the peace treaty with France – even though he didn't really agree with them himself! He only made the speech because the government asked him to, and he thought he owed them a favour after all the honours and decorations they'd showered on him over the years. A lot of his listeners weren't impressed.

How can ministers allow such a fool to speak in their defence?

Of course Emma thought he was the best thing ever to happen to the House of Lords, and made him do his speeches all over again for her when he got home.

I am quite Nelson mad for him again as an orator!

Horatio's hols

Soon after Edmund's death, Horatio decided to get away from it all for a bit. The Hamiltons were going on a visit to Sir William's family estates in Wales, and Horatio decided to tag along. Of course, being Horatio, he ended up turning it into a sort of triumphal tour.

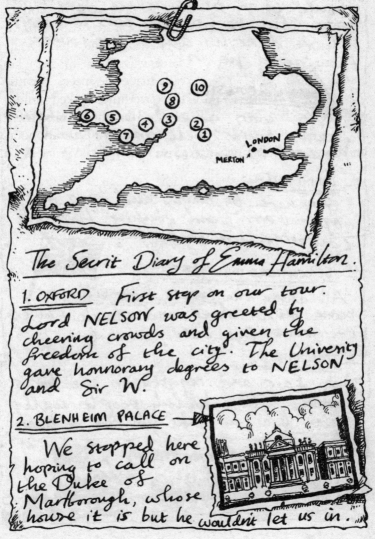

The Secret Diary of Emma Hamilton.

1. OXFORD First stop on our tour. Lord NELSON was greeted by cheering crowds and given the freedom of the city. The University gave honnorary degrees to NELSON and Sir W.

2. BLENHEIM PALACE →

We stopped here hoping to call on the Duke of Marlborough, whose house it is but he wouldn't let us in.

Nice palace though. The Duke's ancestor was given it for defeeting the vile FRENCH. I said my NELSON should be given a palace five times bigger but he said he was just happy to have done his duty to his country. How good he is!

3. ~~GLOSSTER~~ GLOUCESTER

We was greeted here by cheering crowds, bands, bell-ringing and parades of soldiers.

4. MONMOUTH.

Got here by boat, and was met by a brass band playing 'Hail the Conkering Hero Comes'!

5. SOMEWHERE IN WALES.

All along the roads here villagers come out to cheer and chuck flowers as great NELSON passes by.

6. MILFORD.

A fair and regatta in the hero's honner. These Welsh people really know how to make you feel at home.

7. SWANSEA.

Cheering sailors dragged NELSON'S carriage through the streets. He was given the freedom of the town, and made a patriotick speech.

8. HEREFORD.

Getting a bit bored now. When you've seen one cheering crowd you've seen them all.

cheers   huzzah

9. LUDLOW

Much more like it! HUGE crowds gathered outside our inn for a glimpse of NELSON. We was shewn round a china factory and ordered a complete dinner service for Merton and a nice vase with NELSON'S picture on it.

10. BIRMINGHAM

Crowds, factories, banquets etc. Yawn, yawn. Some young women strewed the hero's path with flowers, which was nice.

16th September 1802

Home again to beloved Merton.

Goodbye, Sir William

Horatio had enjoyed his tour. There was nothing he liked better than an adoring crowd, and the crowds in Wales and the West Country still thought of him as the

Hero of the Nile and didn't care about his scandalous affair with Emma. But by the time they returned to Merton, Sir William finally seemed to be losing patience with his wife and her boyfriend.

SHE SPENDS ALL HER TIME WITH LORD NELSON. ALL I WANT IS A BIT OF PEACE AND QUIET, BUT THEY ALWAYS HAVE VISITORS CLUTTERING UP THE HOUSE, AND 12 OR 14 PEOPLE TO DINNER EVERY NIGHT. HEAVEN KNOWS HOW LORD N. CAN AFFORD IT...

IF THEY CARRY ON LIKE THIS, I'LL HAVE TO GO AND LIVE ON MY OWN IN LONDON, AND YOU CAN IMAGINE WHAT A SCANDAL THAT WOULD CAUSE! SO I SUPPOSE I'LL HAVE TO PUT UP WITH IT. I'LL PROBABLY BE DEAD SOON, ANYWAY.

He was right. In April 1803 Sir William finally kicked the bucket. Emma went into deep mourning to show everybody how upset she was.

THICK BLACK VEIL.

FASHIONABLY SHORT HAIR.

BLACK EARRINGS, NECKLACE & BRACELET.

SNIFF!

One of her friends, Madame Vigee Lebrun, described her a few days after Sir William's death.

She said that she was very much to be pitied... She had lost a friend and a father... She would never be consoled. I confess that her grief made little impression on me, since it seemed to me that she was playing a part ... a few minutes later, having noticed some music lying on top of my piano, she took up a lively tune and began to sing it.

TRA LA LA!

Hmmm ... she doesn't sound *all that* upset, does she? She was probably looking forward to spending even more time with Horatio. What she didn't know was that Napoleon was about to stick his oar in again...

COOEE! ALLO, SILLY ENGLISH PIPPLE! REMEMBER ZAT PEACE OF AMIENS? HA HA! IT 'AZ GIVEN ME A NICE BREATHING SPACE TO TRAIN MORE ARMIES AND BUILD SOME 'UGE NEW WARSHIPS! NOW I REALLY AM GOING TO CONQUER EUROPE – AND NUZZING YOUR SOPPY LORD NELSON CAN DO IS GOING TO STURP ME!

WAGGLE

WIGGLE

THRRP!

FOLLOW THAT FLEET

By May 1803 Britain was back at war with France. Nelson was ordered to sea as commander-in-chief of the Mediterranean, and went aboard his new flagship, HMS *Victory*. It was quite an elderly three-decker which had been launched in 1765, and had been Admiral Jervis's flagship at Cape St Vincent – but thanks to Horatio it would soon be one of the most famous ships in the world. Her captain was an old friend, Thomas Hardy, who had been Horatio's first lieutenant at Cape St Vincent, and later one of the 'Band of Brothers' who helped him win the Battle of the Nile.

Horatio was to spend the next two years at sea. At first it was the familiar old job of cruising off Toulon in case the French fleet came out. In good weather it was all right, with officers from different ships rowing across to visit each other and amateur dramatics organized to pass the time, but when storms blew up Horatio suffered terrible bouts of seasickness, which didn't help his temper. As usual, he wrote endless letters to Emma.

Officially, Emma had moved back to her London

home, but she was still spending most of her time at Merton, and sometimes little Horatia stayed there with her. It was still supposed to be a secret that the little girl was her daughter – she had been christened Horatia Nelson Thompson, and officially she was an orphan who Lady Hamilton was just looking after – but at dinner parties aboard the *Victory*, Horatio had his officers drink toasts to Emma and Horatia, so most of them probably guessed who she really was.

The Secret Log Book of H. Nelson

24th August 1803

A terrible thought kept me awake all night! What if Horatia should tumble into the ornamental canal at Merton and drown? I am sure I should go mad if anything happened to her. Must write to Em and tell her to put strong netting around it.

15th September 1803

I think it's time I thought about my precious Horatia's education. Emma's cousin could be her tutoress. At the moment, her official guardian is Mrs Gibson who has looked after her since she was a baby. I think we should make Em her guardian.

2nd February 1804

Letter from my dearest Em.
Apparently the Gibson woman
won't give up Horatia; says she
has grown to love her like her
own daughter! I shall write
and offer her a handsome pension
of £20 per year to let the child
go. If she refuses, she'll get
nothing. Horatia really must
be under Emma's guardianship,
so that she can be properly
brought up and educated. I miss
both of them terribly. Have
thought of asking for sick
leave so that I may go home
and see them, but if I abandon
my post now some other man
will take my place and I might
miss the chance of another
battle.

How I wish the French would
come out and fight! They peek
out at us from Toulon sometimes,
then scurry straight back in, the
cowards.

EEK!

MAMAN!

JE SUIS UN SCAREDY

The French weren't really cowards; they were just being sensible. French Admiral Pierre Villeneuve knew that his men were no match for the experienced Brits. His crews were not as disciplined, and his officers were not as experienced. (A lot of the old French navy's best officers had been aristocrats who had been beheaded or exiled in the revolution.)

Meanwhile, in Paris, Napoleon had decided to give himself a swanky new title.

I'M BORED WIZ ONLY BEING FIRST CONSUL! I DECLARE MYSELF... **EMPEROR OF FRANCE!** GIMME ZAT NICE SHINY CROWN!

He also had a message for the Spanish...

HEY; SPANISH! HELP ME IN MY WAR WIZ ZE STUPID ENGLISH, OR ELSE!

ER...

ALL RIGHT, THEN...

Now Britain was at war with France and Spain again. This was serious. In January 1805 the French managed to sneak out of Toulon, pass the Brit fleet under cover of darkness and escape into the Atlantic. Villeneuve planned to sail to the West Indies, where he would meet up with the Spanish fleet and French ships from the ports of northern France. Then he could sail back with an invincible armada which would smash the Brits in the English Channel and mean that the invasion of England would be on again.

Horatio's fleet chased after the French, eager for a good battle after nearly two years at sea. But when they reached the West Indies, Villeneuve's fleet was nowhere to be seen.

Horatio looked for them at the island of St Lucia, where the British governor told him:

But when he reached Trinidad, Horatio found the French had gone to Martinique after all.

By the time the Brits reached Martinique, Villeneuve had set sail for Europe again; all Horatio saw of the French fleet was three floating planks. The French and Spanish had managed to join up as planned, but the ships from northern France hadn't made it. Hearing that Horatio was hot on his tail, Villeneuve and his Spanish friends scooted back to Europe and nipped into the safety of the Spanish port of Ferrol.

Horatio was as sick as a parrot. He had been hoping for another great victory and all he had got were three planks and a very long wild goose chase. But in a way the hunt for Villeneuve had been one of his greatest achievements. After two whole years at sea, he had led his tired and weather-beaten fleet half way across the world and back. Not many people could have done it. And with Villeneuve cowering in Ferrol, the threat of French invasion was over for the time being.

In August 1805 he finally took a well-earned break, and came home to England. For the last time...

TRAFALGAR

Horatio was afraid that the public would think he was a washout after the flop in the West Indies, and came home half expecting to be mocked, as he had been back in 1798 when he failed to find the French at Alexandria. But nothing could have been further from the truth. Now that Britain was at war again, the country needed heroes – and Horatio Nelson was still the biggest hero of the lot.

He was also one of the first celebrities of the age of mass-production. In the old days a successful general or seaman might get a statue in a public place, but in the new, industrial Britain, where goods could be produced quickly and cheaply, everybody could afford a souvenir of Nelson. There were Nelson mugs and Nelson jugs, Nelson boxes, Nelson fans, Nelson brooches and Nelson hankies.

Print shops sold cartoons of him; not the rude jokes about him and Emma that had been bestsellers a year or so before, but patriotic pics which showed him as 'The Defender of England's Shores'. As for portraits, so many painters and sculptors wanted to make likenesses of him that at one point he was posing for two at the same time, one drawing him from his left and one from his right. This prompted him to make another hilarious joke.

I'm not used to being attacked from both port and starboard...

Well, maybe you had to be there.

In London, Horatio was mobbed and cheered wherever he went, but at Merton Place he was finally able to lead the life he had dreamed of with Emma. He had plenty of visits there from family and friends, and now Horatia was there too. Although she was four and a half by this time, Horatia still hadn't found out that Emma and Horatio were her mum and dad: officially she was an orphan and they were her godparents. Nelson said she was 'a delightful child' and 'very quick' ... but then all mums and dads say that about their own sproglets, don't they?

Horatio seemed more at ease during this time, and not nearly so vain. Perhaps he was a bit more certain of himself and didn't need to keep showing off. One of his nephews said: 'At table he was the least heard among the company and, so far from being the hero of his own tale, I never heard him allude voluntarily to the great actions of his life.'

In the old days Horatio had almost always worn his uniform with all its medals and ribbons. He still dressed like that when he had business in London, but at Merton now he usually changed into civilian clothes.

Down to the sea again...

Horatio only had a few weeks to enjoy Merton. On 2 September a messenger arrived with news from the Channel Fleet.

ADMIRAL VILLENEUVE'S FLEET HAS LEFT FERROL AND TAKEN REFUGE IN CADIZ! MORE THAN 30 FRENCH AND SPANISH SHIPS-OF-THE-LINE!

Horatio knew that this meant that the battle he had been cheated of at Martinique was finally looming. He set about making ready to go to sea again – and before he did, he wanted to make some sort of permanent demonstration of his love for Emma. Obviously they couldn't get married...

OVER MY DEAD BODY!

...but Horatio wasn't going to let a little detail like that stand in his way. He was so sure that God had meant the two of them to be together that he arranged a sort of wedding substitute. He and Emma went to church and took Holy Communion together, then exchanged gold rings in celebration of their 'friendship'.

Emma, I have taken the sacrament with you this day to prove to the World that our friendship is the most pure and innocent.

OH YEAH?

Emma was brokenhearted at losing him again so soon, but she knew she couldn't persuade him not to go. Soon afterwards, he left for Portsmouth, where the *Victory* lay at anchor, and by the end of September Horatio was in the waters off Cadiz, where Admiral Collingwood's fleet was keeping an eye on the French and Spanish. Two days later, on his 47th birthday, he invited 15 of the other captains to a party aboard the *Victory*, and while they were there he told them his plan for flummoxing the enemy when they came out.

THE FRENCH ALWAYS FORM THEIR SHIPS UP IN A LONG LINE. THAT'S JUST WHAT WE WANT! I SHALL SPLIT OUR FLEET INTO THREE DIVISIONS. THE FASTEST WILL STAY IN RESERVE. THE OTHERS WILL GO STRAIGHT AT THE FRENCH LINE HERE AND HERE. BY THE TIME THE SHIPS AT THE FRONT OF THEIR LINE CAN TURN BACK TO HELP, WE WILL HAVE SMASHED THEIR REAR AND CENTRE.

HUZZAH!

BRAVO!

HAPPY BIRTHDAY!

Now it was just a question of waiting for the French to leave Cadiz. But although Villeneuve had 33 ships-of-the-line – the same number as Nelson's fleet – he showed no sign of shifting.

LET'S JUST SIT TIGHT IN ZIS NICE SAFE HARBOUR! I STILL REMEMBER HOW ZAT 'ORRIBLE NELSON TOUGHED US UP AT ZE BADDLE OF ZE NILE! I'M NOT RISKING ANUZZER RUN-IN WITH HIM!

But in Paris, Napoleon was starting to get impatient…

PAH! ADMIRAL VILLENEUVE EEZ LE TWIT SUPREME! LAST YEAR HE FLURFED URP OUR CHANCES OF INVADING ENGLAND – NOW HE EEZ HIDING IN CADIZ! I 'AVE 'AD ENURF OF 'IM! I 'AVE ORDAIRED ANUZZER ADMIRAL TO TAKE OVER AND SAIL INTO ZE MEDITERRANEAN. EEF WE CAN'T INVADE ENGLAND, WE'LL INVADE NAPLES INSTEAD!

Back in Cadiz…

FLIPEEN' ECK! I DON'T WANT TO 'ANG ABURT WAITING FOR SOME UZZER BLOKE TO CURM AND STEAL MY JURB!

ADMIRAL! SIX OF THE BRITISH SHIPS HAVE BEEN SENT AWAY TO FETCH FOOD AND WATER!

HOORAH! ZAT LEAVES THEM WITH ONLY 27 SHIPS! ZIS IS OUR CHANCE! SET SAIL FOR NAPLES AT WERNSE! BUT LET'S TRY AND STEER CLEAR OF ZAT SCARY LORD NELSON, EH?

On 20 October the Brits saw the French and Spanish ships set sail and leave Cadiz. Horatio ordered his ships to steer a parallel course, but not so close that they would scare Villeneuve back into port. All through the night they sailed, and at four o'clock the next morning Horatio ordered a sudden change of course that would bring the two fleets together.

There was no avoiding a ginormous battle now. All night, Horatio had been having his usual premonitions of death. As the French fleet drew closer he asked Captain Hardy and another of his captains, Henry Blackwood, to put their names to a document he had just written...

21st October 1805,
in sight of the combined fleets of France & Spain,
distant about ten miles.

I leave Emma Lady Hamilton ... to my King and Country, that they will allow her an ample provision to maintain her rank in life. I also leave to ... my country my adopted daughter, Horatia Nelson Thompson; and I desire she will use the name of Nelson only.

These are the only favours I ask of my King and Country at this moment when I am going to fight their battle.

It all sounds a bit complicated, but what it boiled down to was that if Horatio got himself killed he wanted the British government to look after Emma and Horatia. Sounds reasonable, doesn't it?

The biggest battle of them all

Now the fleet was almost ready to close with the enemy. Aboard the *Victory* the cannon had been run out of their gun-ports and the gun-crews were standing ready with smouldering tapers, ready to open fire. Horatio decided it was time to send a signal to the rest of the fleet to buck up their spirits.

193

HORATIO'S MESSAGE DIDN'T GO DOWN AS WELL AS HE'D HOPED ABOARD SOME OF THE OTHER SHIPS...

WHAT'S HE SIGNALLING FOR? WE ALWAYS DO OUR DUTY, DON'T WE?

MEANWHILE, HIS OFFICERS WERE GETTING WORRIED ABOUT HIS CHOICE OF OUTFIT.

DON'T YOU THINK A PLAIN BLUE COAT MIGHT BE BETTER, MY LORD? WITH ALL THOSE MEDALS AND DECORATIONS, THE FRENCH SHARPSHOOTERS ARE BOUND TO SPOT YOU...

GLEAM!

DAZZLE!

OH, IT'S TOO LATE TO CHANGE NOW. ANYWAY, THESE ARE MILITARY MEDALS, AND I'M NOT AFRAID TO SHOW THEM TO THE ENEMY.

WHY NOT COME ABOARD MY FRIGATE, SIR? YOU'LL BE SAFER THERE, AND HAVE A BETTER VIEW OF THE BATTLE.

CERTAINLY NOT!

There was no time to argue about it. It was 21 October 1805 and it was about lunchtime. In other words, it was time for...

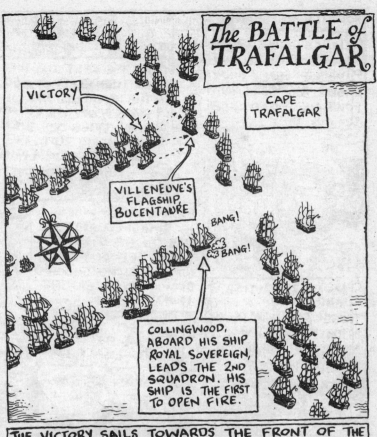

THE VICTORY SAILS TOWARDS THE FRONT OF THE FRENCH LINE, THEN TURNS TO ATTACK THE BUCENTAURE AND ANOTHER FRENCH SHIP, REDOUBTABLE.

By about four o'clock the gunfire started to peter out and Captain Hardy came down to the sick bay to tell Horatio that he had won a brilliant victory and that at least 14 enemy ships had been captured.

Horatio was very weak by that time, but he was still able to give orders. He could feel by the movement of the ship that a storm was on its way, and he told Hardy to anchor. He also asked him not to throw his body overboard, and to look after Emma. Then he said:

Kiss me, Hardy...

Hardy stooped and kissed his cheek. But those *weren't* Horatio's last words. He lived long enough to hear the gunfire stop altogether, while the chaplain and surgeon did their best to make him comfortable. After a while he whispered, 'Remember that I leave Lady Hamilton and my daughter, Horatia, as a legacy to my country. Never forget Horatia.' A few moments later he murmured, 'Thank God that I have done my duty.'

At about half-past four, three hours after the bullet hit him, Horatio died.

NO MORE NELSON

The battle of Trafalgar had been a huge victory. The Brits had lost no ships, but 18 enemy ships had been captured, one had exploded, and the rest were so badly damaged that most of them would never sail again. Napoleon's naval power was smashed, and he now had no hope of controlling either the English Channel or the Mediterranean.

POO! BURM! AND KNICKAIRS!

But a couple of months later he won a stupendous victory of his own, against the Austrian armies at Austerlitz, and it was another ten years before he was finally defeated by the Brits and Prussians at the battle of Waterloo.

There would be other sea battles in the course of the long war, but most of them just involved a couple of ships, or two small squadrons. There wasn't another battle between massed fleets – and there never would be. People were already starting to experiment with steam-powered ships, which would make the sailing vessels of Nelson's day about as much use as a pedal car at the Grand Prix. Trafalgar wasn't just Horatio's final battle: it was also the last great battle of the age of sail.

Soon after the battle ended, the storm which Horatio had predicted struck the fleet. Admiral Collingwood, who was now in command, had ignored Horatio's last order and hadn't bothered to anchor. Now his battered and dismasted ships were scattered by fierce winds and heavy seas. On the captured enemy ships, British crews worked with the French and Spanish sailors they had been fighting a few hours earlier in a desperate struggle to stay afloat. But by the time the weather calmed down a few days later four of the captured ships had been sunk with all hands.

A foul fact and a fittingly fab funeral

Horatio's body was put in a barrel of brandy to stop it going off while the badly battered *Victory* was towed to the British base at Gibraltar. There, it was transferred into a lead coffin filled with spirits of wine – and as a special honour some of his sailors were allowed to drink the brandy.

Meanwhile, the schooner *Pickle* was sent to England with news of the battle. Emma was at home in bed when a messenger from the Admiralty called to let her know what had happened. He didn't have to say anything...

...tears in his eyes and a deathly paleness over his face made me comprehend him. I believe I gave a scream and fell back, and for ten hours I could neither speak nor shed a tear.

Soon the whole country knew about the Battle of Trafalgar. People were overjoyed to hear of Horatio's great victory, but were stunned to learn that he was dead.

THE SOLAR ORB

8th December 1805

NELSON: A NATION MOURNS

As news of the late battle near Cape Trafalgar spreads, people don't know whether to jump for joy or sit down and sniffle.

All over the country, ballads and hymns are being composed in praise of Lord Nelson, who died so heroically at the moment of his greatest victory over the French. The print shops are full of his picture, and plans are underway to collect money for a grand memorial. Streets, squares, ships, pubs, gooseberries, carnations, racehorses and even a prize ram have all been named in Nelson's honour.

Apology: In some of our earlier editions we might accidentally have given the impression that we thought Lord Nelson was a silly show-off with a big, fat girlfriend. He was, of course, the greatest Englishman who ever lived.

The ORB says, GAWD BLESS YA, HORATIO!

London set about getting ready for a funeral fit for a hero. At the beginning of December the *Victory* was towed to Greenwich, where Horatio's body lay in state for three days. Then he was put aboard a barge and rowed upriver by some of his sailors, escorted by black-draped boats and watched by silent crowds along the riverbanks.

Next day, 10,000 troops led the funeral procession through the streets of London to St Paul's cathedral, where Nelson had asked to be buried. (He didn't fancy Westminster Abbey as he had heard it was built on marshy ground and thought it might sink.) The coffin was carried on a special carriage made to look like the *Victory*, and ahead of it marched sailors carrying the

Victory's flag, still full of shot holes from the battle (the flag, that is, not the sailors). The crowds of mourners were so quiet that the only sound as the procession passed was the rustle of the men all taking off their hats.

Inside St Paul's the service went on for four hours before Horatio was finally lowered into his tomb in the crypt, directly underneath the great dome. His black marble sarcophagus was one that had been knocking about at Windsor Castle ever since Henry VIII had it pinched from Cardinal Wolsey 300 years before – nice to know it came in handy at last.

The sailors who had carried the flag were meant to furl it and place it neatly on the coffin, but when the moment came they couldn't bring themselves to do it. Instead they ripped it up and stuffed the bits inside their jackets, as mementoes of their fave admiral.

Sadly, although the Brits spent a fortune on his funeral, they were too stingy to carry out Horatio's last request, and Emma and Horatia never got the government pensions he had wanted. All his titles, as well as £9,000 reward money for Trafalgar and a £5,000-a-year pension, went to his brother William. Will also got an earldom, although he had done nothing to deserve it except have Horatio for a brother. Collingwood said…

Of all the dull, stupid fellows you ever saw, he is the most so.

Horatio's sisters got £10,000 each, and Fanny was granted a pension of £2,000 a year for the rest of her life, but poor

Emma never got a sausage. The government thought she should be content with the money Sir William had left her. They also thought she was a bit of an embarrassment. People wanted to remember Horatio winning battles, not running around after Lady Hamilton. Emma wasn't even allowed to go to the funeral.

In the end, Sir William's money wasn't enough to pay for the sort of life she had in mind. She kept entertaining all her friends and relatives at Merton until the cash ran out, and in 1813 she was put in prison for debt. The following year she took Horatia to live in Calais, where she started drinking heavily, and died in 1815. But even she got a monument in the end. In 1994 an American named Jean Kislak arranged for an obelisk to be erected on the site of Emma's grave in Calais.

Horatia came back to England, where she later married a vicar, had nine children and lived to the ripe old age of 81. She was proud to tell people that Horatio was her father, but she would never admit that Emma was her mum.

Here's to Horatio

Horatio was a hero, not just for a few weeks, but for years and years to come. In a strange way, that French sharp-shooter had done him a big favour. After all, his battles had not all been triumphs; at Tenerife and Boulogne his plans had gone badly wrong, and ended in disaster. He had been vain, often reckless, and sometimes cruel, and

his affair with Emma Hamilton had made him a laughing stock. But because he died at the moment of his biggest success people remember mainly his victories; the Nile, Copenhagen and especially Trafalgar.

Naval officers after Nelson all tried to follow his example, both in the way they fought battles and the way they treated their men, and to this day a toast is drunk to Lord Nelson each year on the anniversary of the Battle of Trafalgar.

Nelson souvenirs are *still* being made and sold, and memorials to heroic Horatio can be found all over the country. Most of them show  him surrounded by figures representing things like Fame and *Victory*. One of the oddest is this Nile memorial in Nottinghamshire, which looks like a Pharaoh's bungalow ...

And one of the nicest is this one at Taynilt, near Loch Etive in Scotland. The iron smelters there had provided the cannon balls for Nelson's fleet, and it was they who dragged this 12-feet slab of granite to the top of a grassy mound and set it upright like an ancient standing stone to mark his death.

The *Victory* ended up as a sort of monument, too. She was kept afloat until 1922, but by then she was in such a bad state that she had to go into a dry dock at Portsmouth. There she was restored to her 1805 condition.

But the most famous memorial of all is Nelson's Column, which was built in London's Trafalgar Square in 1842. Adolf Hitler thought it was such a powerful symbol of Britain that in 1940, when his German armies were planning their own invasion, he plotted to take it home to Berlin as a symbol of his victory – but luckily his invasion plans went the same way as Napoleon's. The column is 45-metre-high, and the bronze panels round the base show scenes from Horatio's battles, made from melted-down French cannon that he

captured. Perched on the top is a 5-metre-high statue of Horatio, looking dead heroic.

Horatio would have been pleased by all the monuments and memorials – but he'd be even more pleased to know that he would still be Horribly Famous 200 years after his great victory.